PENGUIN BOOKS

BRIT SPICE

In 1999 voice-over artist Manju Malhi beat hundreds of other contestants
to secure a guest cookery slot on BBC2's *Food and Drink*. Since then she
has presented her own television show for Taste TV called *Simply Indian*.
*Brit Spice* is her first book and is a winner of a 2002 Gourmand World
Cookbook Award. Manju Malhi lives in London.

# Brit Spice

## Manju Malhi

PENGUIN BOOKS

PENGUIN BOOKS

Published by the Penguin Group
Penguin Books Ltd, 80 Strand, London WC2R 0RL, England
Penguin Putnam Inc., 375 Hudson Street, New York, New York 10014, USA
Penguin Books Australia Ltd, 250 Camberwell Road,
Camberwell, Victoria 3124, Australia
Penguin Books Canada Ltd, 10 Alcorn Avenue, Toronto, Ontario, Canada M4V 3B2
Penguin Books India (P) Ltd, 11 Community Centre,
Panchsheel Park, New Delhi – 110 017, India
Penguin Books (NZ) Ltd, Cnr Rosedale and Airborne Roads,
Albany, Auckland, New Zealand
Penguin Books (South Africa) (Pty) Ltd, 24 Sturdee Avenue,
Rosebank 2196, South Africa

Penguin Books Ltd, Registered Offices: 80 Strand, London WC2R 0RL, England

www.penguin.com

First published by Michael Joseph 2002
Published in Penguin Books 2003
3

Set in Adobe Garamond
Printed in England by Clays Ltd, St Ives plc

To my dad, Yash, who taught me how to follow my dreams.

# Contents

# Introduction

In the sixties my mum and dad left the coastline of Bombay for the shores of Britain. They had little money but wanted to start a new life free from the rigid rules of Indian society. My mother worked as a nurse in Harefield Hospital and my father as a textile chemist. My mother learnt to use all kinds of ingredients that were new to her and often improvised to make cheap and cheerful Indian meals for my father. They were both adventurous and ready to try out different flavours. Even my father loved to cook, and had picked up some skills from his mother in the Punjab. He loved creamy and sweet dishes laden with clarified butter – ghee.

I was born into a loving family, who tried to give me everything, but growing up in Middlesex as an Asian girl had its ups and downs. I was bullied at school because I was different and sought solace in cooking and learning from my mother about Indian food and traditions. I spent a couple of my pre-teen years in Bombay where, at the weekends, we'd travel to the seaside and eat mouthwatering snacks, such as potato cakes with chickpeas and Indian bubble and squeak. Sometimes we'd visit local fast-food restaurants for delicious savoury pancakes and cassata ice cream.

In my home we explored and respected all kinds of grub. My parents taught me not to waste food and to cook only as much as was needed, but that didn't mean starving or eating bland dishes: we conjured up many delicious meals from whatever ingredients were available. I nurtured my passion for food from an early age.

Two years ago I entered a competition on the BBC's *Food and Drink*, which required entrants to send in a home video demonstrating their culinary skills. I decided to prepare a coriander chutney in the garden – an outdoor setting would make it that little bit different, I thought. When it came to filming, it was another matter: there I was in the centre of my weed-infested garden in the middle of January, freezing my socks off while trying to look calm and professional with a howling gale blowing my ingredients everywhere. My poor friend Jane, who was behind the camera, hadn't known what she was letting herself in for! After the fifth take it was time for a wrap and I posted it.

I was thrilled to win the competition, and asked the *Food and Drink* team why they had chosen me. They told me it was the simplicity of my recipe. That's the way I like things, I suppose. Nothing too complicated. So, in this book I have tried to make everything as simple as possible – and also to dispel some of the myths surrounding Indian cooking. Such as:

- It's all hot.
- All Hindus are vegetarian.
- Curry is made out of curry powder.
- Indian food is just curry.

There is no one kind of Indian food. India has twenty-four states and territories, which contain a total population of over 900 million people of different faiths and backgrounds, and more than fifty styles of cooking. Today, the streets of India are full of vendors selling all kinds of food from spicy deep-fried snacks to Chinese dishes. And, of course, Britain's multicultural society is now reflected in the food we cook at home or find in restaurants along our high streets.

Brit-Indi cooking is my way of using British and Indian ingredients in fresh, adventurous, trendy, vibrant, quick and easy dishes – the best of British and the essence of Indian. It's about adding a bit of spice to your life, and is a celebration of two distinct cuisines whose flavours and textures unite in harmony. I've included many of my favourite dishes, such as spicy Cheese on Toast, Ten-Minute Chicken Curry, Fried Mackerel, Coconut and Mustard Chutney, Bread and Butter Pudding with Papaya and Saffron and, of course, Baked Beans Balti.

I'm not a chef and I've never been professionally trained in the art of cooking, but I've dabbled, experimented and created a collection of very quick and very easy recipes that I'd like to share with you. As I've discovered, there are no hard and fast rules to cooking Indian food. It's just a matter of taste.

Over the years, I've tried to find an all-encompassing book on Indian cuisine but failed. I wanted to know how to rustle up quick Indian meals using western ingredients such as white bread, bacon and even Spam! Many Asian households in Britain are familiar with spiced-up baked beans served with chapatis. In the end I improvised and this book contains recipes for some of my favourite concoctions. Over the years I noted down the various dishes my mother prepared so I have also included many authentic recipes for Indian dishes and curries that you might have experienced in Britain's Indian restaurants.

It's well worth investing in a food-processor or blender – chutneys and sauces can be prepared in them in no time at all. Otherwise, if you're a dab hand at chopping and slicing, a sharp knife is just as good. The utensils section (see page xii) gives notes on the best. I've also shown you how to prepare your own blends of spices: they can be bought ready-mixed from the supermarket, but home prepared spices are always fresher and add a personal touch to your cooking.

Often, instead of using traditional Indian techniques, I have found short-cuts, which should suit everyone who lives life in the fast lane.

I have also offered suggestions at the end of many recipes for other dishes to serve at the same time, but these are intended as a guide. It's entirely up to you and what you fancy. I've tried to limit the ingredients in each dish as far as possible. The only long lists will be for spices. Make sure you have your store cupboard stocked up with these (see pages xiii–xxvi) and you can't go wrong. I've also added preparation and cooking times, so that you can plan your meal effectively. Most of the dishes take less than 30 minutes from start to finish – much quicker than waiting for a takeaway!

I do hope that you find this book dispels some of the myths that Indian cooking is hard, time-consuming and painstaking. It really isn't. The most important thing is to have fun.

Enjoy!

# Utensils

A mini guide to knives, gadgets, pots, pans and measuring implements that will make preparation and cooking easier.

**Two good-sized saucepans:** heavy-based, and at least one should have a lid.

**A non-stick frying pan:** to make omelettes, sauté vegetables and dry-roast spices.

**Wooden spoons and spatulas:** cheap to replace and won't scratch non-stick pans. To make your spoons last longer, season them with a coating of oil before you start using them – as you would a brand-new cricket bat.

**A blender and coffee-grinder:** the only gadget I use regularly. It's very handy for puréeing sauces and grinding spices. If I'm going to help a friend cook a meal, I always take it with me.

**A food-processor:** if you want to splash out and also save time you would otherwise spend chopping.

**A sharp knife:** the business. I cannot remember the number of times I've been to a house where the kitchen drawer has countless knives but all blunt and no use to anyone. Knife-sharpeners are not expensive.

**A grater.**

**A good garlic crusher:** useful, but not essential. You can crush garlic with the base of a saucepan.

**A peeler:** choose one that's easy to grip and slides over the contours of irregular-surfaced vegetables.

**A couple of chopping boards:** one for meat, the other for vegetables.

**A colander:** for draining and washing vegetables.

**Tongs:** for turning chapatis.

**Mixing bowls:** for marinating, mixing and storing food.

**A rolling pin:** for making bread and crushing small amounts of whole spices.

**A plastic measuring jug:** with metric and imperial measurements.

**A roasting tin** and **a flat baking sheet.**

If you want to get really serious, get hold of a **kitchen timer.**

# Store Cupboard

I've included a few Indian essentials that I always have available. The dried ingredients keep well for ages and provide the building blocks for some really spicy meals. Ginger, garlic and onions should be stored in a cool place. Keep fresh ingredients, like coriander leaves and chillies, for a few days in the refrigerator.

### Chickpea Flour (Besan)

Chickpea flour is made from ground split chickpeas, or Bengal gram, and is also known as gram flour. It is an earthy yellow colour and has a pleasantly spicy, nutty, fragrant smell. It is used in batter for deep-fried savoury snacks, such as pakoras and bhajis. You can buy it in Asian grocery stores and health-food shops. It should be stored in an airtight container away from sunlight.

### Coconut (Nariyal/Narial)

Coconut, the fruit of the palm tree *Cocos nucifera*, is available all year round. The edible white flesh is surrounded by a hairy hard brown shell. When buying a coconut, shake it to check that the inside contains water, which means it is fresh.
**Cream coconut:** sold commercially as a solid white block, this is the most concentrated form. Available in cans and cartons.
**Desiccated coconut:** unsweetened, dried shredded coconut; used especially in desserts and often in chutneys.
**Coconut milk:** unsweetened, available in cans. Used to increase the amount of curry sauce.
**Coconut milk powder:** the milk, dehydrated and ground to powder. Used to sweeten and thicken curries.

### Garlic (Lasoon)

The dried root of *Allium sativum*, a member of the lily family. It grows in a bulb that consists of several cloves. Processed forms include flakes, powder, salt and purée, but it is best to use fresh whenever possible.

A whole clove gives off only a mild scent but when crushed or chopped releases a powerful, pungent, lingering aroma. It has a sharp and biting flavour. When frying garlic, don't let it burn as it will taste bitter.

In Indian cooking garlic is used in curries, chutneys, pickles, vegetarian and meat dishes. However, some Indians avoid eating root vegetables for religious reasons so they do not cook with garlic. Store in a cool, dry, ventilated place away from light.

### Ghee

Ghee is clarified butter: the clear butter fat is separated from the solids of buffalo (because of the high fat content) or cow's milk. Although there's no real substitute for ghee, butter comes close. Most of the recipes are made with oil and many other Asian households have stopped using ghee in daily cooking because it is so high in cholesterol. Ghee is available commercially but I've explained how to make it on page xxviii.

### Root Ginger (Adrak)

Ginger comes from the same family as turmeric (see page xxvi). It is grown in India and Jamaica. Fresh root ginger is bulbous in shape with a beige skin. It has a creamy yellow and slightly fibrous interior. It smells rich, sweet, warm and woody, and its flavour is biting with a hot note. Root ginger plays an important role in Indian cookery as it's used in almost every meat and vegetable dish. Some Indian households prepare a paste of ginger and garlic and store it in the refrigerator. You can buy it now in supermarkets.

Crystallized ginger can be used to replace fresh ginger: wash off the sugar first if you are preparing a savoury dish. Alternatively, use ground ginger. One teaspoon of the powder is equivalent to 2 teaspoons of grated fresh root ginger. Ground ginger is used in sweet pickles and spicy relishes.

Store root ginger in the fridge, wrapped in kitchen paper and a tightly closed plastic bag. Store ground ginger away from sunlight in an airtight container for up to 6 months.

## Oil (Tel)

Indians use all sorts of oils for cooking depending on which region they come from. People in northern and eastern India use mustard, peanut, groundnut, sesame and rapeseed oils. In the south it's mainly coconut oil. However, in my recipes I have suggested you use vegetable, olive or sunflower oil. Olive oil is very expensive in India and it's only considered as a massage oil!

You can use vegetable oil for deep-frying and for general cooking purposes and olive oil for the more extravagant dishes. If you can get hold of some of the more unusual oils, try substituting rapeseed for olive oil, groundnut or mustard oil for vegetable oil.

## Onions (Pyaz/Piaz)

Onions are the base for most north Indian curries. They're added to virtually every dish to thicken, garnish, flavour or colour. They can be boiled, sautéd, fried or ground to a paste. Use a food-processor, if you have one, to chop a large number. If you're planning to eat onions raw opt for the Spanish variety, which are juicy, mild and sweet.

## Poppadums

Also known as papads, poppadums are an Indian crispbread or savoury wafer usually made from chickpea, or gram flour (see page xiii). There are different regional varieties, some made with rice, potato and even tapioca, and seasoned with garlic, chilli, cumin or black pepper. The flat disc shapes are either deep-fried or grilled, which takes seconds. In Britain's Indian restaurants it has become customary to serve poppadums as a snack with several chutneys before the main course. However, in India they are eaten either with the meal or at the end. Ready-made poppadums, ready to fry or grill, are available in most supermarkets.

## Pulses

In Hindi, pulses are known as dal. They include lentils, beans and peas. Packed with protein, they provide the staple for vegetarian diets. Look out for black-eye beans, butter beans, chickpeas, red lentils, red kidney beans, black lentils, gram lentils, yellow lentils and mung beans. They are used in curries, stuffings, salads, snacks and pancakes, and are available dried or ready-cooked in cans.

## Tamarind (Imli)

The tamarind is an evergreen tree that grows in southern and central India. It bears pods similarly shaped to runner beans. They are brown with a thin brittle shell, and inside is fleshy pulp, which surrounds shiny black seeds. The pulp is mashed with a little water then the juice is extracted and used in cooking. Tamarind is used as a souring agent in curries, and also in chutneys and spicy relishes. It is very good in fish dishes.

There are two forms of tamarind that you might find in the supermarket:

**Tamarind concentrate** is a thick purple-black paste extracted from the pulp of the tamarind. It can be stirred directly into sauces and curries.

**Tamarind paste** is sometimes sold complete with the fibrous husks. Soak a portion of the slab in warm water for 15 minutes, then strain or sieve it to extract the juice.

### Yogurt (Dahi)

Like tamarind, yogurt is also used as a souring agent in Indian cooking and is an invaluable staple in Indian vegetarian cooking. It is also used as a meat tenderizer, a thickening agent and for making desserts. In India many households prepare their own from fresh milk. When you've burnt your mouth with chilli, douse the flames with yogurt, which neutralizes the power of the chilli. Water will not help.

I have suggested ordinary natural yogurt for most of the dishes in this book but you can use thicker Greek-style yogurt for a creamier finish.

# Spices (Masala)

Hundreds of spices are used in traditional Indian cooking, and it is beyond the scope of this book to describe them all, so here I have included the most commonly used ones. Spices come from roots, barks, leaves, stems, berries, fruits and buds of plants. When they are heated their full aroma and flavour are released. Once you get to know them, you'll wonder how you ever managed without them.

### Asafoetida (Hing)

A dried resin gum extracted from the rhizome or taproot of two species of a giant fennel plant. The best comes from Kashmir. It is sold as a resinous gum but is sometimes available as a dry yellow powder. Raw, it has an unpleasant, pungent aroma and tastes extremely bitter. However, cooked, it tastes like fried onions.

It is a popular spice in vegetarian dishes, and is also used as a substitute for onions and garlic, which are prohibited to certain Hindu castes – Jains and Brahmins, who do not eat roots.

Store in an airtight container away from sunlight for up to 6 months.

### Bay Leaf (Tej Patta)

The European bay leaf comes from the sweet bay, a member of the laurel family, but the Indian variety comes from the cassia tree. It is sold dried and is a dull sage colour and fairly brittle. When cooked, Indian bay leaves give off a pungent, warm aroma, and have a mellow but spicy taste.

One or two leaves are enough to scent a dish. They are used mostly in northern Indian cooking, especially in rice and meat dishes. Add them to a panful of lentils while they boil. They are also used in some garam masala or hot spice mixtures. Remove them from a cooked dish before serving, as you would European bay leaves.

Store in an airtight container in a dry, dark place for up to 6 months.

### Caraway Seeds (Siya Jeera)

Caraway is a biennial herb, a member of the parsley family, and is popular in north Indian cooking. The seed is brown, hard and sharply pointed at either end, and tastes of fennel or aniseed.

Caraway can be used to flavour Indian cheeses. It is also used in hot spice mixtures and to flavour meat and rice dishes.

Store it in an airtight container away from direct sunlight.

### Cardamom (Elaichi)

The dried seed pod of a herbaceous perennial of the ginger family, native to south India and Sri Lanka, it is known as the 'queen of spices'. The pods are used either whole or split to release the seeds. Green cardamom has an intense, pungent, sweet scent and flavour and is widely used. The black variety tastes rather medicinal and is used mainly in northern Indian cooking to flavour meat, pulao and rice dishes. It's also an important ingredient in many hot spice mixes or garam masalas.

Store in a cool, dark place. Ground cardamom loses its flavour quickly so buy it in the pod and crush or grind it as you need it.

## Cassia (Jungli Dalchini)

The bark of a tree from the laurel family. China is the largest producer of this spice but it is also grown in north-east India. It is often confused with cinnamon because of its appearance and aroma, which are similar. It tastes strong, woody and bittersweet, with a slightly sharp edge.

In Indian cooking, cassia is substituted for cinnamon, although not in sweet dishes because of its astringent quality.

Cassia is sold either as pieces of bark or as a powder. If a recipe requires cassia powder, don't grind the bark in your coffee-mill. You'll be there all day and the blades will have a tough time.

Store in an airtight container in a cool, dark place for 6 to 12 months.

## Chillies (Mirch)

Chillies are the pods of an annual plant of the capsicum family. There are hundreds of varieties but they all have fire power. Fresh unripe chillies come in various shades of green and in all shapes and sizes. The ripe ones are red and vary according to type in taste and heat. Chillies are always most pungent when raw, and mellow when cooked. When chopping chillies, make sure you don't rub your eyes – they will smart.

Generally large, fat, round, fleshy chillies are milder than small, long, thin, pointy ones. Most of the heat is contained in the seeds and the membrane. The Habañero variety is one of the hottest in the world. The best remedy for chilli burn is yogurt or any dairy produce – not water or lager!

The correct use of red chillies is vital to Indian cooking. If you add too much, the chilli will overpower the other flavours in the dish. The longer chillies are cooked, the hotter the result. When a dish turns out to be too hot add some sugar to temper it.

When you buy fresh chillies, choose the ones with smooth, shiny, unwrinkled skins. Store them in the vegetable compartment of the fridge for up to a week. Whole dried chillies will last for a year if kept in an airtight container in a cool, dark place. The powdered variety loses potency after 6 months and should be stored in an airtight container in a cool, dark place.

| Chilli | Appearance | Heat rating |
| --- | --- | --- |
| Anaheim | Long, large blunt-nosed green or red pods | mild and fruity |
| Jalapeño | Blunt almost oval green pods; smoky nutty flavour. Chipotle is the dried version of a Jalapeño | hot |
| Cayenne | Thin pointed pods, sometimes called finger chillies. Generally green in colour | pungent and hot |
| Bird's Eye | Small, thin, pointy red or green pods | very hot |
| Habañero | Short, wide lantern-shaped orange to red pods | a tropical fruity taste, extremely hot |
| Scotch Bonnet | A close relative of the Habañero – light green, yellow or red | very, very hot |
| Serrano | Chunky, plump red or green pods | mild to hot |
| Bullet | Short plump red or green pods | medium hot |

## Cinnamon (Dalchini)

The peeled and curled inner bark from the slim young stems of a tropical evergreen tree of the laurel family. Cinnamon has a sweet, woody fragrance, either ground or whole. When it is broken or ground, the volatile oils are released giving off their warm, sweet, aromatic and pungent flavours.

Cinnamon is used in cakes and desserts throughout the world. Its sweet-spicy flavour enhances vegetables and fruit, and it is an important ingredient in garam masala.

Buy it in small amounts because, like other spices, it loses its potency after a few months. Store in airtight containers in a cool, dark, dry place.

## Cloves (Laung)

The dried flower bud of an evergreen tree. Cloves come from Madagascar, Brazil, Panang and Sri Lanka, and are native to the Molucca Islands, which are now part of Indonesia. Cloves have a rich, spicy aroma. Their flavour is strong, pungent and sweet. Used in excess, they will overpower other spices.

Cloves are used in rice-with-meat dishes, such as biryanis and pulaos, and in garam masala.

Whole cloves can be stored in an airtight container in a cool, dark place for up to a year.

## Coriander Leaves (Hara Dhania)

A herb in the parsley family, similar to anise. The leaves come from the young plant, *Coriandrum sativum*, and look similar to flat-leaf parsley, but are thinner and lighter green. They are sold in bunches in Indian shops, and smell fruity and vibrant. They have a distinct, strong flavour, of ginger and citrus.

You can use the stems as well as the leaves in Indian dishes, but make sure you wash them thoroughly first to get rid of any grit. They feature in curries, chutneys, soups, sandwich spreads and relishes.

Fresh coriander leaves do not keep well so store them in the fridge, for up to 3 days, in a plastic bag, or with the stems in a glass of water. Discard any wilted or discoloured leaves.

## Coriander Seeds (Dhania)

The seed of the *Coriandrum sativum* plant, a member of the parsley family. It is globular, brown to yellow red, with alternating straight and wavy ridges. It has a mild but distinctive flavour similar to a blend of lemon and sage.

Coriander seeds, whole, crushed or powdered, are used

widely in Indian cooking, and are one of the main ingredients in the many Indian hot spice mixtures or garam masala.

Store whole or ground in a cool, dark, dry place for up to 6 months.

## Cumin Seeds (Jeera)

The seed of an annual herb of the parsley family, and a major constituent of curry powder. Cumin seeds are long and oval, and yellowish-brown in colour. They have an earthy, warm, pungent aroma, and taste pungent, spicy and sweet, with a bitter edge. Dry-roast the seeds lightly to enhance their unique flavour and scent and use them in meat and vegetable curries, spicy salads and yogurt. They are endlessly versatile.

Store in an airtight container away from sunlight for up to 3 months.

## Curry Leaves (Kari Patta)

Curry leaves lend a lingering aroma to a dish, and are discarded before serving. They come from the curry plant, a shrub native to India and Sri Lanka. They are slender, dark green and similar to a small, narrow bay leaf.

The leaves smell fresh and pleasant, remotely reminiscent of tangerines, and add an aromatic curry flavour to any dish. They are the trademark of southern Indian cooking, used to flavour meat, fish, vegetables, lentils, rice and bread. They are also used in preparing Madras curry powders.

If you cannot get hold of fresh curry leaves, try the dried variety. You can buy either from Asian shops. Store fresh ones in the fridge for up to 2 weeks. They can be frozen for 3 months. Store dried ones in an airtight container away from light for up to 6 months.

### Curry Powder (Curry Masala)

Although curry powder is associated with Indian cuisine, it was invented by the British. Throughout the days of the Raj the word 'curry' evolved as a loose description of any Indian food cooked in a hot, spicy sauce. It is not an authentic ingredient in Indian cooking. Spice blends, known as masalas, are mixtures of ground or whole spices native to India, such as turmeric, ginger, chilli, coriander and cumin. They impart a distinct flavour to chicken, fish, meat, vegetables and tea.

Some curry powders are made from up to 30 herbs and spices, while others may contain only 4–5 ingredients. In India, each family has their own recipe, which they make up frequently.

Store curry powder in a dark, glass jar for 2–3 months.

### Fennel Seeds (Saunf)

Fennel seeds are the dried ripe fruit of the perennial herb. They resemble cumin seeds but are green and plumper with yellow ridges. Good quality fennel seeds have a warm, aniseed flavour and aroma, which turns slightly bitter when roasted.

Fennel seeds are used in many Indian spice mixtures to enhance meat dishes and sweeten desserts. It is also one of the ingredients in tea spice or chai masala.

Fennel seeds should be stored away in a cool, dark, airtight container for up to 6 months.

### Fenugreek (Methi)

The seed of an annual herb related to clover. It is small, hard, oblong and dull yellow in colour; ground fenugreek is a warm, yellowish-brown with a bitter flavour that often dominates curry powders. Once it is cooked the flavour mellows.

It is used in a wide variety of spice mixes – for example, sambhar powder, which flavours southern Indian vegetable and dal dishes. Dry-toast fenugreek before grinding or soak it overnight to blend into curry pastes.

Store the seeds or powder in a dry, dark place for up to 6 months.

## Garam Masala

The name means a mixture of spices, and the blending of spices is fundamental to Indian cookery. There are infinite different combinations, and every one imparts its own distinctive flavours. Blends of garam masala vary enormously, according to local or regional tastes. For example, in northern Indian cooking, cardamom, cinnamon, cloves and black peppercorns feature in it, while the Bengali version, of north-east India, *panch phoran*, is rather like Chinese five-spice powder. It contains cumin, nigella, fennel, black mustard and fenugreek seeds.

Each Indian household produces its own unique blend of spices to produce a garam masala and I have included two simple recipes for you to try. However, commercially blended garam masala is available in most major supermarkets. Store garam masala in an airtight container for up to 6 months.

## Mustard Seeds (Rai)

Mustard seed comes from three large shrubs, *Brassica juncea* (brown mustard), *Brassica nigra* (black mustard) and *Brassica hirta* (white mustard). All three produce bright yellow flowers that die off to leave small round seeds. The brown mustard seed is more pungent than the white and is used predominantly in Indian cooking.

Mustard seeds are small, matt, hard, spherical, and either brown, white or black. When heated, they taste bitter, nutty, hot and aromatic. They are a key ingredient in some vegetable dishes and in pickles. In Bengal, they are often ground to make sauces for fish. Cooks in southern India fry a small quantity with other seasonings, such as cumin and curry leaves, before eating them – take care when you do this: the seeds pop in the hot oil and fly about with a life of their own. The spiciness of mustard seeds, no matter how pungent, does not linger, and they impart a rich, earthy taste to any dish.

Store in an airtight container in a cool, dry place for up to 1 year.

## Onion or Nigella Seeds (Kalaunji/Kalonji)

Nigella is grown predominantly in India and is used extensively. Although the seeds are also known as onion seeds they have nothing to do with onions. They are tiny and jet black, a bit like chips of coal, and smell slightly acrid when rubbed between your fingers. They have a nutty, bitter flavour.

Onion seeds are one of the five spices in the Bengali *panch phoran* (see page xxiv), and are also added to naan bread.

Store in an airtight container in a cool, dark place for up to 6 months.

## Paprika (Deghi Mirch)

Paprika comes from sweet, mild peppers and capsicums that are sun-dried then ground to a fine brilliant red powder. It smells and tastes sweet and lightly pungent, then faintly bitter. The combination of turmeric (see page xxvi) and paprika adds the vibrant orange red colour to many Indian dishes.

Store in a dry, dark place for up to 2 months.

## Peppercorns (Kali Mirch)

Native to India, the peppercorn is the king of spices. Black peppercorns are the fermented green berries of a perennial vine plant, *Piper nigrum*, sun-dried to turn them black and hard. Green, white and pink peppercorns are from the same plant as the black variety, picked at varying stages of ripeness. Black peppercorns should be large, even in size and a deep rich brown. They smell earthy, warm and pungent. Their flavour is released on grinding and enhanced by heat. However, once ground, the volatile oils soon evaporate so add pepper towards the end of cooking.

Good-quality black peppercorns will keep for many years in a cool, dark place in an airtight container.

### Saffron (Kesar)

Saffron is the dried red stigma of *Crocus sativus*, an autumn-flowering plant. More than 75,000 crocus blossoms are needed to produce a pound of saffron. It is very expensive but, fortunately, a little goes a long way. It adds a rich golden colour to rice dishes. Saffron is sold as the whole stigmas, wiry strands or threads in a deep vibrant orange or red colour. It should have a strong, penetrating, clinging aroma, and an aromatic, warm rich flavour.

Saffron supplies the characteristic flavour and colour in Indian dessert sauces and milk puddings. Steep the stigmas in water for a few minutes before using them to extract as much as possible of their flavour.

Store wrapped in Cellophane in an airtight container away from sunlight for 2 months. Buy small quantities as it loses its flavour quickly.

### Turmeric (Haldi)

Turmeric comes from the root of *Curcuma longa*, a leafy plant in the ginger family. The roots are boiled or steamed then dried and ground – the most widely available form – to a deep yellow powder. It is mildly aromatic and tastes pungent, bitter and earthy. Don't use it as a substitute for saffron – the colour might be similar but the flavour is entirely different.

Turmeric is one of the most versatile spices in Indian cooking. Its rich orange yellow colour adds to the appearance of any dish, and it is a vital ingredient of curry powder.

Store it in a cool, dark and dry place for up to 4 months.

# How To . . .

Here is a short guide to some of the essential techniques and more fiddly processes involved in Indian cooking.

**Chop Onions**   Cut off both ends of the onion, peel it, then cut it in half lengthways. Place the flat side of one half of the onion on the chopping board and slice it thinly. Then turn it and slice it again, dicing it. The thinner the slices, the finer the chopped onions will be.

To prevent your eyes watering, put a small piece of bread inside your upper lip. Apparently it works!

**Brown Onions Quickly**   Make sure you chop them evenly and small. Add an extra tablespoon of oil to the amount required in the recipe and a tiny sprinkling of sugar.

**Seed and Chop Chillies**   Cut off the stalk and halve the chilli. Scrape out the seeds and the membrane, then hold the chilli on the chopping board with one hand and slice it into tiny rounds with the other. Remember to wash your hands, knife and chopping board thoroughly afterwards. If you would like a finished dish to be very hot, don't discard the seeds.

**Cut Okra**   First wash the okra whole in water, then dry them thoroughly. They must not be damp when you cut them. Then slice off the stalks and chop the flesh into rounds about 2 cms/¾ in thick. Do not wash them after you have cut them up or they will exude a sticky substance.

**Eat with Your Hands**   In India, the left hand is considered unhygienic, as it is used to perform other functions, such as washing, so to eat, use the right hand. Employ the fingertips, never the palm, to scoop up rice and vegetables then mould them into a ball and tip this into your mouth. Bread is eaten in the same way. Tear off enough for a mouthful and wrap some vegetables or meat in it. Eating with your hands gets easier with practice!

**Grind Spices**  Use a pestle and mortar to grind a small amount. Otherwise use an electric coffee grinder. Banish the smell of spices from the machine by grinding rice grains in it for a few seconds to absorb the aroma.

**Make Breadcrumbs**  Toast some bread, allow it to cool for 10 minutes, then grate it into crumbs.

**Make Clarified Butter (Ghee)**  I'm not a great fan of ghee – it's very fatty – and prefer to use oil.
Take some unsalted butter and melt it in a heavy-based pan over a low heat. Let it bubble gently for about 15 minutes. You will notice that the froth disappears leaving a clear yellow liquid. Skim off any froth that remains. When it starts to bubble rapidly, carefully strain and pour the liquid into a heatproof container; set it aside to cool. Throw away the milky residue in the pan. Store it in the fridge for up to 4 months.

**Reduce the Heat in Your Curry**  Cut a lemon in half. Add the juice of one half to your curry, place the unsqueezed ½ lemon in the curry and cook for a few minutes, then remove it.

**Remove Excess Salt from Curry**  Peel a small potato, cut it into chunks, drop it into the curry. Turn off the heat and leave it for 20 minutes. Take out and discard the potato before you continue cooking.

**Slice Mangoes**  Slice off all the flesh around the stone, making 4 pieces of mango. Remove the skin – either slice it off, or push the skin side of the mango until the flesh sticks up, then slice it off the skin.

**Thicken Curry Sauce**   Cook the curry for a little longer with the lid off to allow the water to evaporate, or add ¼ teaspoon of cornflour mixed with a little water and stir over a low heat until the sauce has thickened.

**Use Root Ginger**   Peel off the skin with a knife then chop finely or grate the flesh.

**Wash Rice**   Measure the rice needed and place it in the saucepan you're going to cook it in. Rinse with cold water several times, occasionally rubbing the grains gently in your hands until the water is almost clear. Otherwise, put the rice into a sieve and hold it under the cold tap, moving the rice about until the water runs clear from the rice.

# Food Safety Tips

- Avoid eating foods that are past their sell-by date.
- Red kidney beans may contain harmful toxins which can cause food poisoning so boil them rapidly for the first 10 minutes of the cooking time.
- Store eggs in the fridge, pointed end down and away from strong-smelling foods.
- When handling chillies, avoid touching your eyes or any other part of your body. Wash hands, knife and cutting board thoroughly afterwards. Wear rubber gloves for extra protection.
- When handling spices, avoid touching your eyes and wash your hands thoroughly after use.
- Keep raw and cooked meat separate: harmful bacteria may be easily transferred between them.
- Store raw meat, poultry and fish well covered, on the lowest shelves of the fridge so that they can't drip on to anything else.
- Cool hot dishes to room temperature as quickly as possible before putting them into the fridge or freezer, within 1–2 hours of cooking.

- Avoid overfilling your fridge. Otherwise the temperature may rise to an unacceptable level.
- Check labels on pre-packed food to make sure that it is suitable for home freezing.
- Keep prepared cold foods in the fridge; they should be covered and away from raw foods.
- Put cold leftovers, covered, into the fridge as soon as you have finished eating.
- Wash hands thoroughly before and immediately after handling raw meat.
- Use separate chopping boards, knives and surfaces for raw meat and cooked food, or scrub them thoroughly between uses.
- Frozen poultry must be thawed completely before cooking. Make sure there are no icy crystals left in the cavity and that the legs and thighs move easily.
- Never refreeze food once it has started to thaw.
- Always reheat cooked rice until it is piping hot. If you're in a restaurant make sure that the rice is piping hot all the way through.
- Do not buy damaged cans that have 'blown' or where the ends are bulging.
- Do not store opened canned food in the can. Transfer the contents to another container, then cover and store in the fridge.
- Do not keep food warm. Keep it piping hot or cool it quickly by standing the container in cold water, stirring the contents occasionally and changing the water frequently.
- Do not reheat cooked dishes, whether you've prepared them at home or purchased them, more than once. Reheat them until they are piping hot.

### When you're barbecuing . . .

- Keep raw food away from food that is ready to eat.
- Don't leave perishable food out in the warm air.
- If possible, pre-cook poultry in the microwave or oven, then take it straight to the barbecue to finish the cooking.

- Wash salads and raw vegetables well to remove all traces of soil and any insects.
- Cook burgers, sausages and poultry thoroughly until they are piping hot, the juices run clear and no pink bits remain.
- During cooking, if food starts to burn on the outside before it is done in the middle, raise the grill height.
- Keep serving bowls covered to protect food from dust and insects.
- Eat food as soon as it is cooked.

# Note on Recipes

If at all possible, have all your ingredients and utensils in front of you before you start cooking.

- Preparation and cooking times are approximate timings only.
- Cooking times may vary slightly, depending on individual ovens.
- Use the centre of the oven for baking.
- For fan-assisted ovens, adjust cooking times according to the manufacturer's guidelines.
- Follow either metric or imperial measurements but do not mix them.
- If your microwave oven has a lower or higher wattage, you may need to increase or decrease the cooking time accordingly.

# Spices
# १ मसाले

Spices play an important part in most cuisines but are most prominent in Indian cooking. The secret in preparing good Indian food is to use fresh, aromatic spices. If you're cooking with whole spices, discard them before serving if possible: once they have imparted their flavours to the dish, their job is done.

These days, a vast array of commercially prepared curry powders is available but I have included here some simple spice mixtures to inspire you. Once you have familiarized yourself with a few basic recipes, there'll be no end to the combinations you'll come up with, but do ensure that no individual spice overpowers the others. A few key spices are used in most Indian dishes: cumin, coriander, turmeric, garam masala (a mixture of spices) and chilli powder. The last can be substituted for fresh chillies. I have been known to take a small kit of them with me when I visit friends to rustle up some supper. Curry powder, which was apparently a British invention, can often be substituted for all five spices.

# Manju's Curry Powder

Manju Ka Masala मन्जु का मसाला

Nothing can replace the satisfaction you'll gain from preparing your own curry powder. And when friends taste dishes made with it they'll all want the magic formula to try it out for themselves.

Preparation: 1 minute for blitzing   Cooking: 2 minutes for roasting the spices

| | |
|---|---|
| 6 dried red chillies | 2–3 green cardamoms |
| ¼ tsp black peppercorns | ¼ tsp cumin seeds |
| 5 cloves | ¼ tsp coriander seeds |
| 2 small pieces cassia bark *or* cinnamon | ¼ tsp turmeric |

Heat a heavy-based frying pan, then add all of the spices, except the turmeric, and cook for a couple of minutes to bring out the aroma and flavours, shaking the pan occasionally and being careful not to let them burn.

Remove the pan from the heat and set it aside to cool, then place the spices in a clean coffee-grinder with the turmeric and whiz to a fine powder – you may have to do this in batches depending on the size of the grinder. The ground ingredients will have a pungent smell, so be careful when you open the coffee-grinder. You will need ½–1 teaspoon of this blend to make a dish for 4 people. Store in an airtight container for up to 6 months.

**Tip**
- If you don't have dried red chillies replace them with 1 teaspoon of chilli powder, which you can add after you have ground the whole spices.

# Mum's Hot Spice Mix
Ma Ka Masala मा का मसाला

My mum swears by this and uses it in almost any recipe. She also includes the green husk of the cardamoms in the blend, which adds to the sweetness.

Preparation: 1 minute   Cooking: 2 minutes for roasting the spices

| | |
|---|---|
| 1 tbsp brown *or* white mustard seeds | 8 green cardamoms |
| ½ tsp black peppercorns | 1 tsp fennel seeds |
| 1 tsp cloves | 4 large dried red chillies |

Roast all the ingredients in a frying pan for 2 minutes. Let the spices cool down then blitz them in a coffee-grinder. Store in an airtight jar and use about ½ teaspoon in dishes that serve 4 people.

**Tip**
• Omit the mustard seeds if you don't have any.

# Hot Spice Garam Masala गरम मसाला

North Indians cannot live without this aromatic blend of spices and use it in almost every savoury dish.

---

**Preparation: 2 minutes  Cooking: 2 minutes for roasting the spices**

---

| | |
|---|---|
| 8 whole cloves | 1 tbsp coriander seeds |
| 8 cinnamon sticks | 2 tsp black peppercorns |
| 8 green cardamom pods | 1 tsp black mustard seeds |
| 4 black cardamom pods | 1 tsp brown caraway seeds |
| 1 tbsp cumin seeds | A good grating of nutmeg, about ½ tsp |

Heat a heavy-based frying pan, then add all of the spices and cook for a couple of minutes to bring out the aroma and flavours, shaking the pan occasionally and being careful not to let them burn. Remove the pan from the heat and set aside to cool. Then put the spices into a coffee-grinder and blitz. You may have to do this in batches.

Store in an airtight container for up to 6 months.

### Tips
- If you don't have cumin or coriander seeds, use the powdered forms.
- Sprinkle a dash of garam masala instead of pepper over your chips to spice them up.

# Tea Spice Chai Ka Masala चाय का मसाला

Add a pinch of this combination of spices to your morning brew. You can make a supply to last 3 months but I like to prepare mine fresh each time. See also Spicy Tea on page 175.

| Makes 2–3 cups | Preparation: 1 minute   Cooking: 2 minutes |
| --- | --- |
| ¼ tsp fennel seeds | ¼ tsp ground ginger *or* a small piece |
| 2 cloves | root ginger |
| 2 green cardamoms | |

Coarsely crush the fennel seeds, cloves and cardamoms with a pestle in a mortar or with a rolling-pin, then stir in the ginger. If you wish to keep some tea spice to hand, increase the quantities in the proportions given above, and store in an airtight jar in a cool, dark place.

### Tip
• Store 5–6 cloves, 6 crushed cardamoms and 1 teaspoon of fennel seeds with your teabags for a hint of wintry spice warmth.

# Indian Spice Rub

Desi Masala Rub देसी मसाला रब

An idea I picked up from south-west American cooking, in which spices are rubbed into meat, fish or poultry before roasting. This one makes a great gift for chilli fanatics.

| For 1 whole chicken | Preparation: 3 minutes |
|---|---|
| ½ tsp chilli powder | ½ tsp ground black pepper |
| 1 tsp ground cumin | 1 tsp mustard powder |
| 1 tsp ground coriander | ¼ tsp salt |

Mix all the ingredients in a bowl and store in a cool dark place for up to 3 months.

To use, rub the chicken with the spice mixture, spread it with butter, cover with foil and roast. Half a teaspoon of spice covers 1 chicken breast or about 150 g / 6 oz of meat.

**Tips**

- Place pieces of meat such as chops or chicken legs with the spices in a plastic bag, then close the opening securely and shake to ensure that the meat is well covered.
- Lay a filleted mackerel on a piece of foil, and smother it with 2 teaspoons of the spice rub. Drizzle over a teaspoon of oil and turn the edges of the foil over to make a parcel. Bake in the oven at 180°C / 350°F / Gas Mark 4 for 30 minutes.

# Green Masala Paste
Taaza Hara Masala ताज़ा हरा मसाला

A really easy paste to make with simple fresh ingredients. Many Indians use this in vegetarian dishes but it tastes just as good in a meat or chicken curry. Just add about 2 tablespoons after you've fried the onions, then stir in the meat.

| Enough for 2 curries | Preparation: 10 minutes |
|---|---|
| 50 g / 2 oz coriander, thoroughly washed and chopped | 6 cloves garlic, peeled and crushed |
| 8 green chillies, stalks removed | juice of ½ lemon, *or* 2 tbsp any vinegar |
| 50 g / 2 oz root ginger, peeled and grated | 2 tbsp vegetable *or* olive oil |
| | 1 tsp sugar |
| | ½ tsp salt |

Put all of the ingredients into a blender and whiz to a thick paste. Use as required.

Store for up to 1 week in the fridge in an airtight container.

**Tips**
- Spread 2 teaspoons over a cod fillet and grill or bake for 5 minutes.
- If the machine struggles to blend the mixture, add 2 tablespoons of water.

# Red Chilli Paste

Lal Mirch Ka Masala लाल मिर्च का मसाला

Another great paste for meat or vegetable curries.

| Enough for 2 curries | Preparation: 10 minutes |
| --- | --- |
| 8 dried red chillies | ½ tsp ground ginger |
| ½ tsp garam masala | 1 tsp malt vinegar |
| ½ tsp ground cumin | 2 tbsp vegetable *or* olive oil |
| ¼ ground coriander | ½ tsp paprika |
| 2 cloves garlic, peeled and crushed | ½ tsp salt |

Soak the chillies in 250 ml / 9 fl oz hot water for a few minutes. Then put all of the ingredients, including the water and the chillies, into a blender and whiz to a paste. It should be dark red and fairly thick. Store for up to 1 week in the fridge in an airtight container.

**Tips**
- Add 2 more tablespoons of oil to preserve the paste for a further week.
- Put garlic cloves into a bowl of boiling water for 5 minutes to make peeling easier.

# Spicy Tomato Paste

Taaza Tamatar Masala Paste ताज़ा टमाटर मसाला पेस्ट

Use ripe red tomatoes – it makes a difference.

| Enough for 2–4 curries | Preparation: 10 minutes |
|---|---|

4 fresh tomatoes, chopped

2 green chillies, stalks removed, seeded
and chopped

2 cloves garlic, peeled and crushed

2 tsp peeled and grated root ginger

1 tsp ground cumin

½ tsp salt

1 tbsp lemon juice

2 tbsp vegetable *or* olive oil

Put all of the ingredients, with a little water, into a blender and whiz to a paste.

Store for up to 1 week in the fridge in an airtight container.

**Tip**
• Add 2 more chillies for extra heat.

# Starters and Snacks
# २ हलका नाश्ता

Starters are not usually served at traditional Indian meals in the home, but some Indian households in Britain offer them to set the mood of an evening. I've included some wicked Prawn Pakoras and my favourite Potato and Gram Flour Fritters.

Often after school, my mum would welcome my friends with some savoury hot snacks, which we'd eat with a mug of tea while watching kids' programmes on telly. What bliss, especially during the dark and bitter British winters! Indians traditionally enjoy a wide range of snacks, nibbles and savoury titbits – too many to include all of them in this book. Wherever you travel in India there will always be fast-food snack shops, stalls and hawkers selling the most delectable spicy mouthfuls. They are often served at home when guests arrive or on other auspicious occasions and during religious festivals. You will probably already be familiar with samosas, bhajis and pakoras, but I've included others that use less oil, like Spicy Bread, Lattice Potato Cakes and Indian-Style Bubble 'n' Squeak, that you can prepare whenever you feel peckish. Accompany them with tomato ketchup or Fresh Green Coriander Chutney (see page 125). I eat spicy Scrambled Eggs almost every weekend for breakfast. It's a firm favourite in India, too, where it is eaten with chapatis and lemon pickle.

# Tomato Soup Tamatar Shorba टमाटर शोरबा

Rasam is a hot soup served in southern India. Made from lentils, it's served with plain rice and is really popular among the staunch vegetarians of that region. This version, minus the lentils, is spiked with curry leaves for their lovely lemony flavour.

| Serves 2 | Preparation: 2 minutes   Cooking: 10 minutes |
|---|---|
| 1 × 400 g / 14 oz can tomato soup | 1 tsp vegetable *or* groundnut oil |
| 6–7 black peppercorns | 6–8 curry leaves (optional) |
| 1 tsp cumin seeds | 2 red chillies, stalks removed, seeded |
| 1 tsp tamarind, seeded and sieved | and cut into 4 |
| (optional) | 1 sprig fresh coriander, washed and |
| 2 tsp brown sugar | finely chopped |

Pour the soup into a saucepan, and put it over a low heat. In another pan, roast the peppercorns and cumin seeds until they release their aroma, then coarsely grind with a rolling pin or with a pestle in a mortar. Stir the powder into the soup, with 125 ml / 5 fl oz water. Turn the heat up to medium, and bring to the boil. Add the tamarind and sugar, and boil gently for 3 more minutes.

In a separate pan (you can use the one you cooked the spices in), heat the oil and carefully add the curry leaves and red chillies. When they splutter tip them into the soup. Remove the soup from the heat, take out the chillies and discard them. Pour the soup into bowls, sprinkle it with the coriander and serve with crusty or garlic bread.

### Tips
- If you cannot get hold of fresh red chillies, try dried ones or a pinch of chilli powder.
- If you cannot find fresh curry leaves, use dried ones. Bay leaves are not a substitute.
- If you can't find tamarind, use 2 teaspoons of lemon juice.

# Lentil and Vegetable Soup
Dal Sabzi Shorba दाल सब्जी शोरबा

When I'm feeling low or too tired to think about what to cook, this is a great pick-me-up. You can try all sorts of vegetable combinations: it's up to you! It's full of fibre and protein with a dash of spice. A meal in itself!

| Serves 2–4 | Preparation: 10 minutes   Cooking: 20 minutes |
|---|---|

| | |
|---|---|
| 1 carrot, peeled and sliced | 1 courgette, sliced |
| 1 potato, peeled and diced | pinch of garam masala |
| 1 onion, peeled and chopped | 1 tbsp red lentils, washed |
| ¼ tsp ground cumin | ½ tsp salt |
| 5–6 cauliflower florets | 1 green chilli, slit lengthways and |
| 2 mushrooms, sliced | seeded (optional) |
| 1 clove garlic | 1 tbsp butter |
| 2.5 cm / 1 in piece root ginger | 1 fresh tomato, halved |

Throw all ingredients into a saucepan and pour in 1 litre / 35 fl oz hot water from the kettle. Bring to the boil over a high heat, which shouldn't take more than 2 minutes, then simmer until the lentils are soft. Serve with toast or bread and butter, or a white roll.

**Tip**
- Substitute 500 ml / 18 fl oz vegetable or chicken stock for the same quantity of water for extra flavour.

# Clear Spicy Chicken Soup

Murg Masala Shorba मुर्ग मसाला शोरबा

If you're recovering from an illness or feeling a bit run down, this soup is nourishing, easy to eat and comforting. It is also prepared in Indian households to treat coughs, colds and flu. The ginger and garlic soothe the throat, while the cloves and peppercorns add warmth.

| Serves 2 | Preparation: 5 minutes   Cooking: 12 minutes |
|----------|----------------------------------------------|

| | |
|---|---|
| 1 roasted-chicken carcass | 1 tsp butter |
| A few slices of onion | 2 cloves |
| 1 clove garlic | 2 black peppercorns |
| 2.5 cm / 1 in piece root ginger | |

Put the chicken carcass, the onion, garlic and ginger into a saucepan with 500 ml / 18 fl oz water, bring to the boil and continue to boil for 10 minutes. Turn off the heat and strain the stock into a bowl. Discard the bones, onion and flavourings.

Take another saucepan – or wash the one in which you boiled the bones – heat it, then put in the butter, cloves and black peppercorns. Fry for 1 minute then pour in the stock. Check the seasoning, then serve hot in a mug or soup bowl.

**Tip**
- Garnish with chopped fresh green coriander leaves if you're serving as a starter as part of a meal.

# Prawn Pakoras Jhinga Pakora झीन्गा पकोडा

This recipe is a lighter variation of Onion Bhajis. Serve them as a party snack or as a starter.

| Serves 2–4 | Preparation: 7 minutes | Frying time: 7 minutes |
| --- | --- | --- |

Vegetable oil for deep frying, approximately 500 ml / 18 fl oz

1 small onion, peeled and finely chopped

1 tsp lemon juice

100 g / 4 oz gram (chickpea) flour

¼ tsp chilli powder

50 g / 2 oz fresh coriander, washed and finely chopped

¼ tsp ground cumin

½ tsp turmeric

¼ tsp sodium bicarbonate

¼ – ½ tsp salt

250 g / 8 oz peeled prawns, defrosted if frozen

Heat the oil in a deep saucepan. In a bowl mix all the ingredients apart from the prawns. Stir well until you have a stiff, sticky mixture. Add a couple of tablespoons of water if the mixture seems too dry, then fold in the prawns. The mixture should be quite stiff and thick.

Check whether the oil is hot enough to start frying. Drop a tiny bit of the mixture into the oil: if it sizzles fiercely the oil is ready.

Slowly place teaspoon-size drops of the pakora mixture into the oil, 5–6 at a time, depending on the size of the pan, and fry for a couple of minutes until they are golden yellow. Remove them and put them on kitchen paper to absorb the excess oil. Taste one and adjust the seasoning of the batter if necessary, then cook the rest.

Serve hot with Tomato and Chilli Chutney (see page 130). The Prawn Pakoras can be reheated in the oven at 160°C / 325°F / Gas Mark 3 for 10 minutes, or in the microwave for 1 minute.

## Tips
- Add 1 clove of crushed garlic and 1 teaspoon of grated ginger for additional flavour.
- Use cauliflower florets, aubergine slices or spinach leaves instead of prawns.

# Lattice Potato Cakes
Ragda Pattice रगडा पेटिस

A dish from Gujarat, Mumbai and the north of India. It's a street food, like hot dogs or fish and chips in Britain. The potato cakes go well with Chickpea Curry (see page 101) – or baked beans!

| Makes 6 potato cakes, to serve 2–3 | Preparation: 5 minutes<br>Cooking: 6 minutes |
| --- | --- |

| | |
| --- | --- |
| ¼ tsp salt | 3 potatoes, peeled, boiled and mashed |
| 25 g / 1 oz fresh coriander leaves,<br>   thoroughly washed and chopped | 2 tbsp rice flour<br>1 tbsp vegetable *or* olive oil |

Stir the salt and coriander leaves into the mashed potatoes. Wet your hands slightly and roll the mashed potato into golf balls. Spread the rice flour over a plate, then flatten the balls to become patties and coat them with the flour.

Heat a frying pan and put in the oil. Sauté the potato cakes for 3 minutes on each side until they are crisp and light golden in colour. Serve immediately.

### Tip
• If you haven't got rice flour, use breadcrumbs.

# Potato and Gram Flour Fritters

Aloo Pakora आलू पकोड़ा

My mum's friend Joyce Robins from Jersey loves these. And they are very moreish.

| Serves 2 | Preparation: 7 minutes   Frying: 8 minutes |
|---|---|

| | |
|---|---|
| Vegetable oil for deep-frying (approximately 500 ml / 18 fl oz) | ¼ tsp chilli powder |
| Pinch of coriander seeds, slightly crushed | ¼ tsp salt |
| | 25 g / 1 oz gram (chickpea) flour |
| Pinch of turmeric | 150 g / 6 oz potatoes, peeled and thinly sliced |
| ¼ tsp cumin seeds | |

Put the deep-frying oil into a saucepan and set it on the hob to heat.

In a bowl, mix together the spices and salt with the gram flour. Add 50 ml / 2 fl oz water and stir it into a thick paste. Drop a few potatoes into the batter and roll them around to coat them in it.

Check that the oil is hot enough: with a spatula, let a drop of oil fall into the batter: if it splatters or pops, it is ready. Drop the coated potato slices into the oil and fry for a few seconds, then turn them to cook the other side. Lift them out on to some kitchen towel to absorb the excess oil. Repeat until all the potato slices are cooked. Serve as snacks with ketchup or any of your favourite chutneys.

### Tips
- You can use chopped green chillies instead of chilli powder.
- Use the leftover hot oil to fry some poppadums, then store them in an airtight container.

# Crab Sticks with Sesame and Garlic
Til Aur Lasoon Ka Kekda तिल और लसुन का केकडा

I love eating seafood sticks on their own but this dish is irresistible. Although it's meant to serve 4, I could easily wolf down the lot!

| Serves 2–4 | Preparation: 3 minutes   Cooking: 7 minutes |
|---|---|

| | |
|---|---|
| 2 tbsp vegetable *or* sunflower oil | 250 g / 8 oz crab or seafood sticks |
| 1 onion, peeled and finely chopped | 2 tsp light soy sauce |
| 2 red chillies, seeded and finely chopped | 1 tsp sesame oil |
| 2 cloves garlic, peeled and crushed or finely chopped | 25 g / 1 oz fresh coriander leaves, washed and chopped |

In a frying pan, a wok or a saucepan heat the oil, and fry the onion for a couple of minutes. Then add the chillies and garlic, and continue to fry, stirring, for a minute. Tip in the crabsticks and cook for a couple of minutes, until they have broken up, then fold in the soy sauce and sesame oil. Garnish with the coriander leaves and serve in a pitta pocket, or as a starter with rocket leaves and watercress.

**Tip**
- If you haven't got red chillies use ¼ teaspoon of chilli powder.

# Curried Eggs Anda Masala अन्दा मसाला

My mum made this when we couldn't be bothered to go shopping. It's really quick to cook and delicious.

| Serves 2 | Preparation: 6 minutes | Cooking: 13 minutes |
|----------|------------------------|---------------------|

| | |
|---|---|
| 2 tbsp vegetable *or* sunflower oil | ½ tsp ground coriander |
| 2 knobs butter (optional) | ¼ tsp turmeric |
| 1 onion, peeled and finely chopped | ¼ tsp chilli powder |
| 4 hard-boiled eggs | Salt |
| ½ tsp ground cumin | Pinch of garam masala |

Heat the oil and the butter in a saucepan then fry the onions for 8 minutes until they are golden brown.

Meanwhile, shell the eggs, quarter them, put them into a bowl and stir them with the cumin, coriander, turmeric, chilli powder and salt. When the onions are ready, tip the eggs into the pan with them and sauté for a few seconds. Sprinkle over the garam masala. Serve hot with chapatis or hot buttered toast.

### Tips
- Plunge a knife into cold water before slicing hard-boiled eggs and the yolk won't crumble.
- This dish makes a great sandwich filler.
- Add a few sprigs of fresh coriander for a bit of colour.

# Peppered Prawn Cocktail पेपर्द प्रोन कोकटेल

Even today many of my friends and family from India talk of this great British classic with affection. It's so different from Indian food, and the flavours are so distinctive that I've only added a touch of heat to it.

| Serves 2 | Preparation: 10 minutes |
|---|---|

Leaves of 1 little gem lettuce, washed

12–14 cucumber slices, halved

½ red onion, peeled and thinly sliced

200 g / 7 oz peeled prawns

4 tbsp mayonnaise

1 tbsp tomato ketchup

1 tsp lemon juice

½ green chilli, seeded and very finely chopped

Pinch of chilli powder

Arrange the lettuce leaves in 2 deep bowls. Mix together the cucumber and onion slices, then pile half of the mixture into each bowl. Sprinkle over the prawns. Stir together the mayonnaise, tomato ketchup, lemon juice and green chilli, and spoon over the prawns. Sprinkle with a tiny amount of chilli powder and serve.

**Tip**
• Use paprika rather than chilli powder for a less spicy result.

# Cheese on Toast Cheese Toast चीज़ टोस्ट

I love this as a snack or for lunch with a hot chilli pickle. I've also introduced my friends to this recipe – my international-food-lover friend Neil impresses his mum and his mates with it.

| Serves 2 | Preparation: 6 minutes   Cooking: 4 minutes |
|---|---|

2 slices bread

1 small tomato, finely chopped

½ small onion, finely chopped

100 g / 4 oz grated Cheddar cheese

1 tbsp fresh coriander, washed and chopped

Pinch of ground cumin

Knob of butter

Lightly grill the bread on both sides or place in a toaster on a medium setting. Meanwhile, stir together the remaining ingredients in a bowl. Spread the cheese mixture evenly over one side of each slice of toast. Make sure the toast is completely covered. Place it under the grill until the cheese bubbles and lightly browns. Serve immediately with ketchup.

**Tip**
- If you have no coriander leaves, add a pinch of chilli powder instead.

# Scrambled Eggs Anda Bhurji अन्डा भुरजी

Indian meat-eaters love this dish and eat it for breakfast or lunch with chapatis! Normally the eggs are laden with lots of spices but I've kept the flavours to a minimum, with just a bit of fresh green chilli and coriander.

| Serves 1 | Preparation: 3 minutes   Cooking: 7 minutes |
|---|---|

| | |
|---|---|
| 2 eggs | 1 green chilli, seeded and chopped |
| 1 tbsp milk | 1 small tomato, finely chopped |
| Pinch of salt (optional) | 25 g / 1 oz fresh coriander, finely |
| Knob of butter | chopped (optional) |
| ½ onion, peeled and finely chopped | |

Break the eggs into a bowl, add the milk and the salt then whisk with a fork for a few seconds. Heat the butter in a saucepan, then fry the onion and chilli for a couple of minutes to soften them. Then add the tomato and continue to fry for 2 more minutes. Pour the egg mixture into the pan, add the coriander then stir continuously until the eggs are nice and fluffy – not too runny but not rubbery either. Serve immediately with some buttered toast.

**Tip**
- Add a couple of chopped mushrooms to the softened onion.

# Indian Omelette Desi Omelette देसी ओमलेट

At the crack of dawn in India's railway stations men and women armed with eggs and frying pans are to be found preparing these omelettes outside carriage windows. It's a great spectacle to watch and makes travelling on India's railway network all the more fun.

| Serves 1 | Preparation: 3 minutes   Cooking: 2 minutes |
|---|---|

2 eggs

½ onion, peeled and finely chopped

1 green chilli, seeded and finely
  chopped

1 tbsp fresh coriander, finely chopped

Pinch of salt

Pinch of black pepper

1 tbsp vegetable *or* sunflower oil

1 fresh tomato, finely chopped, for
  garnish

Whisk together all of the ingredients except the oil and the tomato in a bowl with a fork. Heat the oil in a frying pan. Carefully pour the omelette mixture into the pan and cook for 30–45 seconds, then flip over the omelette and cook on the other side. Serve, scattered with the chopped tomato, and with some bread or toast.

## Tips
- Grate a bit of cheese over the omelette before serving.
- If you have no fresh chillies, put in a little extra black pepper.
- Add some diced cooked potato to the egg mixture.

# Indian–Style Bubble 'n' Squeak
Pau Bhaji पाव भाजी

This snack is sold in shacks around the beaches of Mumbai. It's a great fast food dish and very popular among Indians. For convenience and speed, I have used frozen vegetables. Don't be tempted to use oil rather than butter – the result won't taste as good.

| Serves 4 | Preparation: 7 minutes   Cooking: 26 minutes |
|---|---|

| | |
|---|---|
| 1 large potato, peeled and diced | 1 kg / 2 lb 3 oz mixed frozen peas, |
| 125 g / 5 oz butter | carrots and cauliflower, defrosted |
| 1 onion, peeled and finely chopped | 400 g / 14 oz can tomatoes or fresh |
| 4 green chillies, seeded and chopped | tomatoes, chopped |
| ½ tsp turmeric | 8–10 soft white snack rolls |
| 1 tsp ground coriander | A few sprigs fresh coriander, washed |
| 1 tsp ground cumin | and coarsely chopped |
| ¼ tsp salt | |

Microwave the potato on high for 5 minutes.

Heat 100 g / 4 oz of the butter in a saucepan or wok, and fry the onion and chillies for 5 minutes. Add the turmeric, coriander, cumin and salt and fry for another minute. Add the mixed vegetables – not the potatoes – to the pan. Cover and continue to cook gently over a low heat for 5 minutes.

Then, mash the vegetables coarsely in the pan. Add the tomatoes, replace the lid and continue to cook gently for 2½ minutes. Then mash the vegetables a little more. Cover again and cook for another 2½ minutes. Then add the potato, cook for a couple of minutes and mash again. The mixture should look fairly dry and – wouldn't you know? – coarsely mashed. Add a knob of butter, mix and set aside the pan.

Heat a griddle or a fairly flat frying pan. Slice the bread rolls in half and spread them with the remaining butter (you can leave out the butter, if you prefer). Place the rolls, butter side down, on the griddle and heat for 2 minutes on either side. Put a couple of tablespoons of the vegetable mixture on each piece of roll. Scatter over the coriander and serve.

### Tips
- Can also be used as a sandwich filling the next day.
- For speed, blitz the tomatoes in a blender.
- Defrost the frozen vegetables in the microwave if you're short of time.

# South Indian Semolina Uppama अुपमा

This dish is so simple yet full of the flavours of south Indian cooking.

| Serves 2–4 | Preparation: 3 minutes   Cooking: 12 minutes |
|---|---|

| | |
|---|---|
| 250 g / 8 oz semolina | 4 curry leaves |
| 2 tbsp groundnut *or* vegetable oil | 1 tsp skinned split black lentils |
| ¼ tsp mustard seeds | ½ onion, peeled and chopped |
| Pinch of asafoetida (optional) | 1 potato, peeled and diced small |
| ¼ tsp turmeric | ¼ tsp salt |
| 1 dried red chilli | |

Heat a saucepan and put in the semolina. Stir well for about 5 minutes to roast it, but don't let it burn. Its colour should darken only a little. Take it off the heat and set it aside.

In another saucepan, heat the oil and add the spices and black lentils. Stir-fry until the seeds begin to crackle and pop. Put in the onion, the potato and the salt and continue to fry for a couple of minutes. Then add 500 ml / 18 fl oz water to the mixture and cook for 5 minutes or until the potato is nearly done. Tip in the semolina and cook for a further 5 minutes or until the potato is soft. Serve with lime pickle (available from supermarkets) or natural yogurt.

### Tips
- To save a little time, parboil the potato in advance.
- Try 100 g / 4 oz green peas instead of potato.

# Spicy Bread Tarka Bread तड़का ब्रेड

Another quick-to-prepare, and tasty, lunch or supper dish. You can make it several hours before you plan to eat it, and warm it up in the microwave.

| Serves 2 | Preparation: 5 minutes   Cooking: 10 minutes |
|---|---|

| | |
|---|---|
| 2 tbsp vegetable *or* olive oil | ¼ tsp salt |
| ¼ tsp mustard seeds | 1 tbsp yogurt |
| 1 small onion, peeled and sliced | 1 tsp lemon juice |
| 2 green chillies, seeded and chopped | 4 slices bread, cubed |
| ¼ tsp turmeric | Fresh coriander leaves, to garnish |
| ½ tsp sugar (optional) | 1 tomato, chopped |
| ¼ tsp ground cumin | |

Heat the oil in a saucepan, then add the mustard seeds. Once they have popped, tip in the onion and chillies and stir for a minute. Then add the turmeric, sugar, cumin and salt and continue to fry for 1 minute. Pour in the yogurt and lemon juice, stirring continuously. Lastly, fold in the bread carefully so that it doesn't crumble too much. Cook for 2 more minutes, then serve sprinkled with coriander and chopped tomato.

**Tip**
• Dollop some extra yogurt over the finished dish to cool it.

# Chicken and Poultry
३ मुर्ग़

As Hindus don't eat beef and Muslims don't eat pork, Indian non-vegetarian fare centres on chicken, fish, lamb and goat. And while Indian Muslims are expert in preparing lamb dishes, Hindus reign supreme in the art of cooking chicken.

In India chicken is expensive so it is generally served on special occasions, and in an infinite variety of dishes – braised, stewed, dry-fried, roasted or grilled. It is also marinated in spicy yogurt mixes for cooking in the *tandoor*. The recipe I've included for Tandoori Chicken doesn't have the regulation red colour with which we're all familiar. Instead, the marinade includes fresh green coriander leaves and chillies for a natural appearance.

Chicken is so versatile and goes with almost any combination of spices you care to throw into the pan with it, and most dishes taste better the day after they are made when the flavours have had time to mingle and the meat has absorbed them.

# Ten-Minute Chicken Curry and Spicy Salad

Dus Minute Ki Murg Curry दस मिनट की मुर्ग करी

The first time I made this in ten minutes I did it to win a bet! However, I had all the ingredients and utensils laid out in front of me, which saved a lot of time – and I chopped the chicken into very small pieces. You can use leftover cooked chicken or turkey, which is even quicker.

| Serves 2 | Preparation: 5 minutes | Cooking: 10 minutes |
| --- | --- | --- |

*For the Chicken Curry*

3 tbsp olive oil

1 medium onion, peeled and sliced

400 g / 14 oz chicken fillets, skinned and chopped

2 cloves garlic, crushed *or* chopped

1 green chilli, seeded and chopped

¼ tsp salt

¼ tsp turmeric

½ tsp ground cumin

¼ tsp ground coriander

1 tsp tomato purée

¼ tsp garam masala *or* 1 tsp curry paste

2 tbsp double cream

*For the Spicy Salad*

1 tbsp olive oil

¼ tsp ground black pepper

½ green chilli, seeded and very finely chopped (optional)

Pinch of salt (optional)

½ tsp runny honey

1 tbsp balsamic *or* cider *or* wine *or* malt vinegar

1 packet mixed green salad leaves

Heat the oil in a frying pan, then put in the onion and fry for 1 minute. Add the chicken and continue to fry for 5–6 minutes. Stir in the garlic and chilli and continue to fry, stirring from time to time.

While the mixture is browning, make up the salad dressing. Take an empty jar with a lid and put in the olive oil, black pepper, chilli, salt, honey and vinegar. Screw on the lid and shake.

Now add the salt, turmeric, cumin and coriander to the chicken mixture. Stir well and continue to fry. Add the tomato purée and garam masala or curry paste, then fold in the cream.

Put the salad leaves into a bowl, shake the dressing again, then pour it over the leaves and toss. Serve the chicken beside a pile of salad, or push everything into pitta bread pockets.

**Tip**
- Use ¼ teaspoon of chilli powder instead of the green chillies.


# Jubilee Curry जुबली करी

I discovered this dish when I was on holiday in Rajasthan. I ordered it in a restaurant in the Pink City of Jaipur. It was so delicious, rich and creamy, and not too chilli hot. I asked the chef the main ingredients and had to guess the rest! It goes beautifully with freshly baked naan bread (see page 115) and basmati rice. A dish fit for a queen.

| Serves 2 | Preparation: 6 minutes   Cooking: 19 minutes |
|----------|-----------------------------------------------|

| | |
|---|---|
| 3 tbsp groundnut *or* olive oil | ½ tsp ground cumin |
| 1 onion, peeled and chopped | ¼ tsp paprika |
| 2 cloves garlic, crushed *or* finely chopped | ½ tsp ground coriander |
| | ¼ tsp salt |
| 1 tsp root ginger, peeled and grated | 2 chicken breasts, skinned and chopped |
| 1 red chilli, seeded and finely chopped | ¼ tsp garam masala |
| ¼ tsp turmeric | 200 ml / 7 fl oz can coconut cream |

Heat the oil in a saucepan, add the onion and fry for 3–4 minutes. As it begins to brown, add the garlic, ginger and chilli, fry for 3 minutes, then add the turmeric, cumin, paprika, coriander and salt, and continue to fry for 1 minute. Stir the mixture well so that it doesn't burn. It should turn thick and aromatic. Put in the chicken and fry gently for about 4 minutes. The onion and spice mixture should smother it. Stir in the garam masala and coconut cream, cover the pan and simmer for 4 minutes. If the sauce seems too thick, add 125 ml / 5 fl oz water. The oil should surface on the top. Serve with plain rice.

# Chicken Balti Murg Balti मुर्ग बाल्टी

Balti means 'bucket' in Hindi so the vessel in which it is cooked has given its name to this buttery dish. In Britain balti houses are thriving in the Midlands and the north, where these hot curries are served in their mini wok-shaped vessels with naan bread.

| Serves 4 | Preparation: 5 minutes   Cooking: 16 minutes |
|---|---|

| | |
|---|---|
| 75 g / 3 oz butter | ½ tsp ground cumin |
| 1 onion, peeled and chopped | ¼ tsp ground coriander |
| 2 cloves garlic, peeled and crushed | ¼ tsp garam masala |
| 2 green chillies, seeded and chopped | 100 g / 4 oz tomatoes, chopped |
| ¼ tsp turmeric | 400 g / 14 oz chicken breasts, skinned |
| ¼ tsp ground fenugreek | and chopped |
| 2 black cardamoms (optional) | 2 tsp peeled and grated root ginger |
| 2 pieces cassia bark *or* cinnamon | 25 g / 1 oz fresh coriander leaves, |
| ¼ tsp salt | washed and chopped |

Heat the butter in a deep saucepan or a medium-sized wok. Add the onions, garlic, chillies, turmeric, fenugreek, cardamoms and cassia bark or cinnamon, then fry for 5 minutes. Add the salt, cumin, ground coriander, and the garam masala. Stir for a few seconds then tip in the tomatoes. Cook the mixture until it begins to thicken. Then add the chicken pieces and cook for 3 minutes. Pour in 250 ml / 9 fl oz just-boiled water. Simmer for 6 minutes until the sauce has reduced again. It should be reddish-brown in colour. Stir in the root ginger, then sprinkle over the coriander leaves. Serve hot with naan bread (see page 115) or plain basmati rice.

### Tips
- You can use ghee (see page xxviii) for extra richness instead of butter.
- If you have no fenugreek, you can use onion seeds instead or leave it out altogether.

# Chicken Dhansak Murg Dhansak मुर्ग धन्सक

A dhansak is made with lentils and a mixture of vegetables or meat. Many dhansak recipes contain a variety of pulses such as yellow lentils (*toor dal*), black lentils (*urad dal*), red lentils (*masoor dal*) and mung beans. You can use any combination of lentils or beans or add just one type, as I've done here. Tiger Woods wannabe Arun is so obsessed with Chicken Dhansak that he has to order it in every Indian restaurant he visits.

| Serves 2–4 | Preparation: 7 minutes   Cooking: 16 minutes |
|---|---|

50 g / 2 oz butter

1 onion, peeled and chopped

2 cloves garlic, peeled and sliced

2 green chillies, seeded and chopped

¼ tsp salt

¼ tsp turmeric

½ tsp ground cumin

¼ tsp ground coriander

2 chicken breasts, skinned and chopped into equal 2.5 cm / 1 in pieces

400 g / 14 oz can green lentils (drained and washed)

1 tbsp peeled and grated root ginger

1 tsp double cream

Melt the butter in a saucepan and add the onion, garlic and chillies then fry for 6 minutes. Add the salt, turmeric, cumin and coriander, and stir for 30 seconds. Tip in the chicken and sear it for 4 minutes, then add the lentils and fry them for 1 minute. Pour in 125 ml / 5 fl oz water, cover and simmer for 3 minutes. Mix in the ginger. Swirl in the cream, then serve with plain rice and a vegetable dish such as Butter Spinach (see page 69).

### Tips
- Use a can of mixed pulses for a nuttier flavour.
- Add a few chopped vegetables after you've seared the chicken.

# Chicken Jalfrezi Murg Jalfrezi मुर्ग जलफ़्रेज़ी

This is my version of a dish that's served up in countless British Indian restaurants. It's a great combination, with the chicken picking up the flavours of the peppers.

| Serves 2–4 | Preparation: 5 minutes   Cooking: 17 minutes |
|---|---|

2 tbsp olive oil

1 onion, peeled and chopped

2 cloves garlic, peeled and sliced

1 green chilli, seeded and chopped

2 tsp curry powder *or* paste

¼ tsp salt

1 tsp tomato purée

2 chicken breasts, skinned and
    chopped into bite-size pieces

1 tsp peeled and grated root ginger

1 green pepper, seeded and sliced

Heat the oil in a saucepan, put in the onion, garlic and chilli and fry for 4 minutes. Add the curry powder or paste, salt and the tomato purée. Stir for 30 seconds then put in the chicken. Sear it for 3 minutes, then add 125 ml / 5 fl oz water. Stir, add the ginger and green pepper and cook for 1 minute. Serve with hot naan (see page 115) or chapatis (see page 117).

### Tips
- For more sauce, add an extra 125 ml / 5 fl oz water and cook for 3 minutes longer.
- Use 2 tablespoons of butter instead of oil for extra richness.

p.5 & p.165 | Tea Spice and Almond Biscuits

p.17 | Potato and Gram Flour Fritters

p.19 | Curried Eggs

p.21 | Cheese on Toast

p.28 Ten-Minute Chicken Curry and Spicy Salad

p.32 | Chicken Jalfrezi

p.38 | Masala Roast Chicken

# Chicken Korma with Beer

Sharaabi Murg Korma शराबी मुर्ग कोर्मा

Indians do not use beer in cooking, but although diehard curryholics may scorn the idea, it tastes good! It adds a bittersweet flavour to the chicken, which is quite delicious.

| Serves 2 | Preparation: 6 minutes | Cooking: 20 minutes |
| --- | --- | --- |

| | |
| --- | --- |
| 2 tbsp vegetable oil | ¼ tsp salt |
| 1 onion, peeled and chopped | 2 chicken breasts, skinned and chopped |
| 2 cloves garlic, peeled and sliced | 150 ml / 6 fl oz Cobra beer |
| 1 green chilli, seeded and chopped | 1 tsp tomato purée |
| ½ tsp turmeric | 1 tbsp cream |
| ½ tsp ground coriander | 1 tsp peeled and grated root ginger |
| 1 tsp ground cumin | ¼ tsp garam masala |
| 1 green cardamom, crushed | |

Heat the oil in a deep saucepan or wok, put in the onion, garlic and chilli then fry for 6 minutes. Stir in the turmeric, coriander, cumin, cardamom and salt. Then add the chicken and fry for 5 minutes. Slowly pour the beer over the meat and cook gently for 5 minutes. Stir in the tomato purée, cream and ginger then take the pan off the heat. Sprinkle over the garam masala and serve with naan bread (see page 115) and a crisp green salad.

### Tips
- If you'd like more sauce, add a few tablespoons of water with the beer.
- If you use a different variety of beer, select one with a sweetish flavour.

# Chicken Tikka Masala

Murg Tikka Masala मुर्ग तिक्का मसाला

I couldn't possibly prepare a British Indian cookbook without including this recipe. You won't find it on a menu in India, though. It was created for the western palate – a mild curry concoction made up of tomatoes and cream.

| Serves 2 | Preparation: 7 minutes, plus 1–2 hours marinating time<br>Cooking: 20 minutes |
| --- | --- |

| | |
| --- | --- |
| 2 tbsp curry *or* tandoori paste | 1 medium onion, peeled and chopped |
| 2 tbsp natural yogurt | 2 red chillies, seeded and chopped |
| 2 chicken breasts, skinned and chopped | ¼ tsp turmeric |
| | ¼ tsp paprika |
| 3 tbsp single cream | ¼ tsp salt |
| 200 g / 7 oz can tomatoes | ½ tsp ground cumin |
| 2 tsp peeled and grated root ginger | ½ tsp ground coriander |
| 2 cloves garlic, peeled and chopped | ¼ tsp garam masala |
| 3 tbsp olive oil | 25 g / 1 oz fresh coriander leaves |
| 2 bay leaves (optional) | (optional) |

Put the curry or tandoori paste into a bowl with the yogurt, stir well, then add the chicken pieces and stir again. Put the bowl into the fridge for 1–2 hours.

Preheat the oven to 180°C / 350°F / Gas Mark 4. Put the chicken pieces into an ovenproof dish and bake for 10 minutes. Meanwhile, blend together the cream, tomatoes, ginger and garlic in a bowl and set it aside.

Heat the oil in a saucepan, add the bay leaves (if using) and the onion and fry until the onion begins to turn golden-brown. Add the chillies, turmeric, paprika, salt, cumin, coriander and garam masala and stir for 1 minute. Put in the chicken pieces and fry for 5 minutes. Then add the tomato and cream mixture, cover and cook over a low heat for a further 5 minutes. The curry should look red and creamy, and its texture should be thick and fairly smooth, depending on how small you chopped the onions. Add 125 ml / 5 fl oz water and cook for another minute. Take it off the heat, pour it into a serving dish and garnish with the coriander leaves. Serve hot with pulao rice (see page 109), pitta or naan bread (see page 115).

# Tandoori Chicken with Coriander
Hara Dhana Tandoori Murg हरा धना तन्दुरी मुर्ग

This has become so popular with my friends that I make it often during the summer. Tandoori cooking is native to the Punjab in northern India: the food is marinated then cooked in giant earthen or clay ovens. The combination of the charcoal and the mixed spices in the marinade gives the food a distinctively 'barbecued' flavour.

| Serves 4 | Preparation: 30 minutes   Cooking: 20 minutes |
|---|---|

| | |
|---|---|
| 4 chicken breasts, skinned and pierced with a fork | 4 cloves garlic, peeled and crushed |
| | ½ tsp ground cumin |
| *For the marinade* | ½ tsp ground coriander |
| 1 tbsp vegetable *or* olive oil | ¼ tsp garam masala |
| 4 tbsp natural yogurt | ½ tsp turmeric |
| Juice of ½ lemon | ½ tsp chilli powder *or* 2 dried red |
| 1 tsp tomato purée | chillies |
| 2 green chillies, seeded | 25 g / 1 oz fresh coriander |
| 2 tsp root ginger, peeled and grated | ¼ tsp salt |

Place all the ingredients for the marinade in a blender and whiz until smooth – the consistency should be fairly thick. Put the chicken into a bowl and pour over the marinade then leave it in the fridge for at least half an hour – the longer you keep the chicken in the marinade the better it will taste.

Remove the chicken from the marinade. Grill, barbecue or bake it until it is thoroughly cooked – the juices will run clear when you stab it with a knife or fork. Serve hot with pitta bread and a fresh green salad with onion rings and mango chutney.

# Cumin Chicken Jeera Murg जीरा मुर्ग

One evening my brother Meno came home late and somewhat the worse for wear. Rather than scoffing the hot curry that traditionally follows a few bevvies, he reheated and ate this mild, delicately spiced dish. Cumin is known to be gentle on the stomach . . .

| Serves 2 | Preparation: 5 minutes, plus 15 minutes' marinating time<br>Cooking: 16 minutes |
|----------|---------------------------------------------------------------------------------|

2 chicken breasts, skinned and cut into bite-size pieces

2 tsp lemon juice

1 tbsp yogurt

¼ tsp salt

1 tsp ground cumin

¼ tsp ground coriander

¼ tsp chilli powder

2 tbsp vegetable *or* olive oil

1 onion, peeled and finely chopped

1 clove garlic, peeled and crushed

In a bowl, mix the chicken pieces with the lemon juice, yogurt, salt, cumin, coriander and chilli powder. Cover and refrigerate for 15 minutes.

Heat the oil in a pan then fry the onions and garlic for 6 minutes until the onions are lightly browned. Add the marinated chicken and sauté for 8 minutes. Then add 2 tablespoons of water and cook for a further 2 minutes. Serve in a tortilla wrap.

**Tip**
- For an even milder flavour, fold in 2 tablespoons of cream at the end of cooking.

# Garlic and Ginger Chicken

Lasooni Adrak Murg लसुनी आद्रक मुर्ग

This is a really simple dish that my mum rustles up when she has unexpected guests or when she doesn't feel like cooking. It's very garlicky, full of flavour and not too spicy.

| Serves 4 | Preparation: 6 minutes   Cooking: 15 minutes |
|---|---|

| | |
|---|---|
| 2 green chillies, seeded and chopped | 4 tbsp vegetable or olive oil |
| 2 tbsp root ginger, peeled and grated | 2 onions, peeled and chopped |
| 4 cloves garlic, peeled and crushed | ½ tsp garam masala |
| 1 tbsp lemon juice | ¼ tsp turmeric |
| 4 chicken breasts, skinned | ¼ tsp salt |

If you have a blender, whiz the chillies, ginger and garlic with the lemon juice into a paste. Otherwise stir them together in a bowl. Put in the chicken pieces and leave them to marinate for a few minutes.

Heat the oil in a large saucepan and fry the onions for 6 minutes until they are caramelized or nice and brown. Stir in the garam masala, turmeric and salt, then add the chicken and cook, still stirring, until the oil surfaces, which should take about 4 minutes. Pour in 125 ml / 5 fl oz water, cover and simmer for 3 more minutes. The colour of the dish should be a light to dark brown, depending on how brown you cooked the onions, and the sauce will be fairly coarse. Take it off the heat, pour off the oil, if you like, and serve with naan (see page 115) or plain basmati rice.

**Tip**
- If you haven't any fresh garlic, use 2 teaspoons of garlic paste.

# Masala Roast Chicken

Masala Chicken Roast मसाला चिकन रोस्ट

My brother is usually rather fussy about my cooking but I got a thumbs-up for this dish! He and I love it. You can use the same ingredients to baste a whole chicken for a Sunday roast, but if you do, cook the potatoes and other vegetables plainly – the meat has all the flavour you need.

| Serves 2 | Preparation: 10 minutes   Cooking: 30 minutes |
| --- | --- |

| | |
| --- | --- |
| 4 chicken thighs with skin, pierced | ¼ tsp ground cumin |
| 2 cloves garlic, peeled and crushed | Pinch of chilli powder *or* 1 green chilli, |
| 2 tsp peeled and grated root ginger | seeded and chopped |
| ¼ tsp salt | 1 tbsp tomato purée |
| Juice of ½ lemon | |

Preheat the oven to 200°C / 400°F / Gas Mark 6.

Place the chicken thighs in a bowl. Stir together the rest of the ingredients, then rub the mixture over the thighs thoroughly. Lay them on a baking tray and roast for 30 minutes. Take them out of the oven and serve with mashed potato or hot pitta breads.

**Tip**
• If you don't have any tomato purée, use a tablespoon of ketchup instead.

# Chicken with Cumin, Sage and Onion

Jeera, Salvia Aur Pyaz Ki Murg

जीरा सल्विया और प्याज की मुर्ग

The flavours of cumin and sage blend well together – and both plants are known to have curative properties.

| Serves 2 | Preparation: 7 minutes   Cooking: 15 minutes |
| --- | --- |

2 tbsp oil

2 medium onions, peeled and chopped

8–10 fresh sage leaves, washed and chopped

¼ tsp salt

¼ tsp ground cumin

200 g / 7 oz can passata (sieved tomatoes)

2 chicken breasts, skinned and chopped

Heat the oil in a frying pan and sauté onions for 3 minutes, then add the sage and stir. Add the salt and cumin, sauté for a few seconds and stir in the sieved tomatoes. Add the chicken and cook for 10 minutes or until it is done – the juices should run clear when you stab it with a knife or fork.

Serve with crusty rolls and green salad.

### Tips

- If you can't find fresh sage, use 2 teaspoons of dried sage instead.
- If you can't find passata, use a 200 g / 7 oz can of plum tomatoes.

# Cumin Chicken Wings

Jeera Murg Kay Tookray जीरा मुर्ग के टुकडे

This marinade has few ingredients and can be thrown together in no time. I've used chicken wings but drumsticks and thighs work equally well.

| Serves 4 | Preparation: 4 minutes | Marinating: 2 hours | Cooking: 20 minutes |
| --- | --- | --- | --- |

| | |
| --- | --- |
| 4 tsp ground cumin | 4 cloves garlic, peeled and crushed |
| 4 tbsp natural yogurt | 8 large chicken wings with skin, |
| ¼ tsp salt |     pierced with a fork |

In a bowl large enough to take the chicken wings, mix together the cumin, yogurt, salt and garlic. Add the wings and coat them thoroughly with the marinade. Cover the bowl with a plate or clingfilm and leave to marinate in the fridge for 2 hours or more – overnight, if you have time. Grill or barbecue the chicken for about 6 minutes on either side until the juices run clear when you stab it with a knife or fork. Or you could roast it in a preheated oven at 200°C / 400°F / Gas Mark 6 for 20 minutes.

**Tip**

- To spice up the flavour, add ¼–½ teaspoon of chilli powder to the marinade.

# Football Vindaloo फुटबोल विन्डाल्

This dish is brilliant because the preparation time is short and the curry will be ready at half-time so you won't miss any of the action. It's a recipe for those who hate fiddly techniques and are lazy in the kitchen, which includes me. Traditionally a vindaloo is made with garlic and wine or vinegar, but it has evolved into something totally different in Britain – a very hot very spicy scorcher of a dish.

| Serves 3–4 | Preparation: 7 minutes   Cooking: 1 hour, including the oven time |
|---|---|

| | |
|---|---|
| 3 tbsp olive or vegetable oil | 2 tbsp hot curry paste |
| 4 onions, peeled and roughly chopped | ¼ tsp salt |
| 8–10 chicken drumsticks, skinned and pricked | ½ tsp chilli powder (optional) |
| | 2 tsp tomato ketchup |
| 4–6 cloves garlic, peeled and chopped or crushed | Knob of butter |

Preheat the oven to 200°C / 400°F / Gas Mark 6.

Heat the oil in a saucepan large enough to hold the chicken and the onions. Tip in the onions, the drumsticks and garlic, and sauté for 7–8 minutes. Put in the curry paste, salt and chilli powder, then stir for 1 minute. Mix in the tomato ketchup with 500 ml / 18 fl oz just-boiled water. Finally add the butter. Transfer the vindaloo to a roasting tin or casserole dish. Loosely cover it with foil and place it in the centre of the oven for 45 minutes. Serve with chips, crusty bread, naan (see page 115) or rice.

### Tips
- You can use tomato purée instead of tomato ketchup.
- If you're not a fan of drumsticks, use any other chicken pieces.
- Cook the chicken in its skin, and pull it off before serving.

# Chicken Liver Masala
Murg Kaleji Masala मुर्ग कलेजी मसाला

This was the only way my mum could get me to eat liver! It's great with plain mashed potatoes, but it also makes a fancy starter served on toasted crusty bread.

| Serves 4 as a starter or 2 as a main course | Preparation: 7 minutes<br>Cooking: 16 minutes |
| --- | --- |

| | |
| --- | --- |
| 2 tbsp vegetable *or* olive oil | ¼ tsp ground coriander |
| 1 onion, peeled and sliced | ¼ tsp garam masala |
| 2 green chillies, seeded and chopped | 400 g / 14 oz chicken livers, picked |
| 2 cloves garlic, peeled and crushed | over and any green bits discarded |
| 2 tsp tomato purée | 2 tsp peeled and grated root ginger |
| ¼ tsp salt | 25 g / 1 oz fresh coriander leaves, to |
| ½ tsp ground cumin | garnish |

Heat the oil in a frying pan and sauté the onions with the chillies and garlic for about 3 minutes.

While the onions are frying, mix together the tomato purée, salt, cumin, coriander and garam masala with about 5–6 tablespoons of water. Add it to the frying-pan and stir for 1 minute, then put in the chicken livers and cook for 5 minutes until they are brown on the outside but still pink in the middle. Lastly, add the ginger and fry for 1 minute. Scatter over the coriander leaves, and serve with pitta bread, hot mango or lime pickle and a Cucumber Raita (see page 123).

**Tip**
- If you prefer chicken livers well done, cook them for a further 5 minutes.

# Hot Chicken Liver Pâté

Masala Murg Kaleji Ki Chatni

मसाला मुर्ग कलेजी की चटणी

There are so many pâtés available in supermarkets but I've never found one with Indian spices or chillies – so I decided to experiment. This is surprisingly good and a great way to eat liver, which is an invaluable source of iron.

| Serves 2–4 | Preparation: 10 minutes Cooking: 4 minutes |
| --- | --- |

100 g / 4 oz butter

250 g / 8 oz chicken livers, picked over and any green bits removed

¼ tsp chilli powder (optional)

4 cloves garlic, peeled and crushed

2 tsp peeled and grated root ginger

1 tsp Madras curry powder

1 tsp malt vinegar

Melt 25 g / 1 oz of the butter in a frying pan and add the chicken livers. Sauté them for 2 minutes. Then add the chilli powder, garlic, ginger, curry powder and vinegar, and stir for a further 2 minutes. The livers should look brown on the outside and dark pink in the middle. Place the mixture in a food-processor or blender. Put the remaining butter into the hot pan and let it melt. Then pour it into the blender, and whiz everything to a fine paste. Spoon the mixture into 2 ramekins or a small terrine, and serve with toast or crusty bread. It will keep in the fridge for 4–5 days.

**Tip**
- If you haven't got any vinegar, use 1 teaspoon of lemon juice.

# Turkey Curry
Paan Murgi Ki Curry पान मुगी की करी

Although turkey takes slightly longer to cook than chicken you could substitute it for chicken in the other recipes in this chapter, such as the Jalfrezi and the Masala Roast. Or what about a Turkey Tikka Masala!

| Serves 4 | Preparation: 5 minutes   Cooking: 22 minutes |
|---|---|

| | |
|---|---|
| 2 tbsp olive *or* vegetable oil | ¼ tsp turmeric |
| Knob of butter (optional) | ½ tsp chilli powder |
| 600 g or 4 turkey breast steaks, | ¼ tsp ground cumin |
| chopped into bite-size pieces | ¼ tsp ground coriander |
| 2 onions, peeled and chopped | ¼ tsp salt |
| 2 cloves garlic, peeled and crushed | 1 tsp tomato purée |
| ¼ tsp garam masala | 2 tsp peeled and grated root ginger |

Heat the oil in a frying pan, add the butter (if using) and fry the turkey pieces for 8 minutes or until they are lightly browned. Remove them from the pan, throw in the onions and garlic and sauté for 6 minutes. Add the garam masala, turmeric, chilli powder, cumin, coriander and salt, then stir well. Pour in 125 ml / 5 fl oz water, stir in the tomato purée and the ginger, then the turkey. Cover and simmer over a low heat for 4 minutes. Serve with brown pitta breads and Butter Spinach (see page 69).

### Tips
- Use leftover roast turkey: add it after you have put in the spices.
- For more gravy, add 50 ml / 2 fl oz extra water.

# Duck Curry Badak Curry बतख करी

This is a very old recipe of my grandmother's. It comes from Goa where duck is popular and the curries are very hot. I've reduced the number of chillies in this recipe, but feel free to add more if you like!

| Serves 2–4 | Preparation: 6 minutes   Cooking: 23 minutes |
|---|---|

| | |
|---|---|
| 2 tbsp groundnut *or* olive oil | 1 tsp ground cumin |
| 1 onion, peeled and finely chopped | 1 tsp ground coriander |
| 4 cloves garlic, peeled and crushed | ¼ tsp salt |
| 2 bay leaves (optional) | 1 tbsp vinegar |
| 2 boneless duck breasts, skinned and chopped | 2 tsp peeled and grated root ginger |
| | 2 tbsp coconut powder *or* |
| 4 dried red chillies | 150 ml / 6 fl oz coconut milk |
| ½ tsp turmeric | Pinch of garam masala |

Heat the oil in a saucepan with a lid, then fry the onions, garlic and bay leaves for 6 minutes. Add the duck and continue to sauté for about 7 minutes until the duck has browned. Put in the chillies, then the turmeric, cumin and coriander. Mix well, then add the salt, vinegar and ginger and stir again.

If you are using coconut powder, mix it with 250 ml/9 fl oz just-boiled water and add it, or the canned coconut milk, to the pan with the garam masala. Cover and simmer for 2 minutes. Serve with plain basmati rice.

### Tip
- If you fancy more sauce add 125 ml / 5 fl oz water when you add whichever variety of coconut you have decided to use.

# Lamb and Other Red Meat
# ४ मटण

The most commonly eaten red meat in India is goat (*bakra*), but high in the state of Jammu and Kashmir, the climate is cooler and sheep are reared. In those northern regions, even Hindus eat meat. Indians use the word 'mutton' to describe lamb and goat meat. Any cut can be used in Indian dishes and is cooked until it is very tender. In some of the recipes that follow, you can substitute beef for lamb but if you do this make sure you extend the cooking time.

Apart from lavish curries, meat also features in succulent kebabs, a Muslim speciality that stems from a Moghul tradition. They are prepared either from minced or small strips of tender meat. Kebabs are usually served dry but can sometimes be converted into a curry by adding spices and yogurt. The minced-meat kebabs are known as Seekh Kebabs and Shammi Kebabs. The former are grilled or roasted, and the latter usually deep fried as a patty. Pasanda Kebabs and Hussaini Seekh Kebabs are well known, made from whole pieces of meat.

If you're not into kebabs, Minced Lamb with Peas is popular in India, as well as in Britain, and quicker to prepare than other meat dishes.

Pork is not so widely available in India but the Goanese know a thing or two about it: they like it hot and spicy in dishes such as Pork Vindaloo. And Spam – yes! – is great when it's spiced and eaten with chapatis and a hot lime pickle.

# Mumbai Hot Lamb Curry

Mirch Wali Mutton Ki Curry मिर्च वाली मटण की करी

In India, the further south you travel the hotter the food becomes. My grandmother used to make this for get-togethers with her friends. They ate it with rice, pooris (see page 118), sautéd cauliflower and carrot chutney.

| Serves 2–4 | Preparation: 16 minutes    Cooking: 45 minutes |
|---|---|

| | |
|---|---|
| 400 g / 14 oz casserole lamb, trimmed and cut into bite-size pieces | 1 tsp curry paste |
| | 1 tsp ground cumin |
| 2 large onions, peeled and finely chopped | 1 tsp ground coriander |
| 200 g / 7 oz can peeled plum tomatoes | 2 dried red chillies *or* ½ tsp chilli powder |
| 4 cloves garlic, peeled and crushed | |
| 1 tsp peeled and grated root ginger | ¼ tsp salt |
| ½ tsp turmeric | |

Boil the kettle. Then put all of the ingredients into a saucepan with a lid, plus 500 ml / 18 fl oz hot water. Cover it and cook over a high heat for 15 minutes. Turn down the heat to medium and cook for a further 15 minutes until the lamb is tender. Remove the lid and continue to cook for 10–12 minutes: the sauce will reduce and thicken. Serve hot with naan (see page 115) and a crisp green salad.

**Tip**
- Replace the tomatoes with a 200 g / 7 oz can of coconut cream for a sweeter, milder curry. Add it after the lamb has cooked over a high heat for 15 minutes.

# Minced Lamb with Peas
## Keema Mattar कीमा मटर

This dish is a good one for the summer. Just fill pitta pockets with the mince and some salad and you're on your way to a delicious picnic snack. It tastes even better the next day.

| Serves 2–4 | Preparation: 6 minutes   Cooking: 21 minutes |
|---|---|

| | |
|---|---|
| 3 tbsp vegetable *or* olive oil | 1 red tomato, chopped |
| 1 medium onion, peeled and chopped | ¼ tsp salt |
| 2 cloves garlic, peeled and sliced | 500 g / 1 lb 2 oz minced lamb |
| 2 green chillies, seeded and chopped | 1 tsp peeled and grated root ginger |
| ¼ tsp ground coriander | 150 g / 6 oz peas, defrosted |
| ½ teaspoon ground cumin | ¼ tsp garam masala |
| ¼ tsp turmeric | |

Heat the oil in a saucepan, then add the onion, garlic and chillies and fry until the mixture begins to turn golden brown, about 5 minutes. Slowly mix in the coriander, cumin, turmeric, tomato and salt and let it sizzle for a minute. Then tip in the mince and brown it for 7–8 minutes, stirring frequently. Add the ginger and continue to fry for 30 seconds. Fold in the peas and cook for a further 4 minutes. Sprinkle over the garam masala, and serve hot with pitta breads.

### Tips
- You can use this mixture as a filling for meat samosas.
- If you have no fresh tomatoes, use 1 teaspoon of tomato purée instead.
- No fresh chillies? Use ¼ teaspoon of chilli powder instead.

# Karahi Lamb Mutton Karahi मटण कडाही

A *karahi* is an Indian cooking vessel similar to a wok in which you can flash fry vegetables and small pieces of meat.

| Serves 2 | Preparation: 2 minutes    Cooking: 19 minutes |
| --- | --- |

2 tbsp groundnut *or* vegetable oil

1 medium onion, peeled and sliced

250 g / 8 oz saddle of lamb, trimmed and cut into thin strips, *or* leg steaks, trimmed and cubed

1 tsp Green Masala Paste (see page 7) *or* Red Chilli Paste (see page 8)

¼ tsp salt

Heat the oil in a wok or large frying pan, then tip in the onions and fry for 5 minutes until they are soft. Then add the lamb and fry over a medium–high heat for 5–6 minutes (or 8 minutes if you like it well done), stirring occasionally. Add the paste and the salt and continue to fry, stirring, for a few minutes. Serve immediately in hot pitta breads or with a Vegetable Pulao (see page 110) and Raita (see page 123).

### Tips

- If you fancy some sauce with this dish, mix 2 teaspoons of tomato purée with 250 ml / 9 fl oz water and add it to the fried lamb, then cook for a few minutes to allow the flavours to mingle.
- Add extra Green Masala Paste for a spicier dish.
- If you have no masala paste, substitute 1 chopped green chilli, ½ teaspoon of grated ginger and 1 clove of crushed garlic.

# Lamb Biryani Mutton Biryani मटण बिरीयानी

This dish is from Hyderabad. I remember stopping off once at a small restaurant on the way to a hill station called Lonavala near Mumbai and ordering a biryani for lunch. It was the best I had ever tasted.

| Serves 4 | Preparation: 30 minutes, includes lamb cooking time<br>Cooking: 20 minutes, for baking the biryani |
|---|---|

| | |
|---|---|
| 2 tbsp gram lentils – *chana dal* (optional) | 3–4 saffron strands (optional) |
| | 2–3 tbsp milk, warmed |
| 400 g / 14 oz casserole lamb *or* 4 chump chops | 1 tsp peeled and grated root ginger |
| | 2 cloves garlic |
| 2 cloves | 4 green chillies, stalks removed, seeded and chopped |
| 2 × 5-cm / 2-in lengths cassia bark or cinnamon sticks | 2 tbsp vegetable oil, plus a little extra |
| 2 black cardamoms | 2 medium onions, peeled and sliced |
| 2 green cardamoms | 250 ml / 10 fl oz natural yogurt |
| 3 bay leaves | 400 g / 14 oz basmati rice, cooked |
| ¼ tsp salt | 2 tbsp butter, melted |
| ½ tsp cumin seeds | Juice of ½ lemon |

Soak the gram lentils in 250 ml / 9 fl oz water for 30 minutes.

Meanwhile, boil the lamb in 500 ml / 18 fl oz water with the cloves, cassia bark or cinnamon sticks, black and green cardamoms, bay leaves, salt and cumin seeds for 20 minutes, until the meat is tender. Keep checking the pan to make sure it doesn't boil over. When it is ready, drain it and discard the liquid and spices.

Soak the saffron in the milk.

Preheat the oven to 180°C / 350°F / Gas Mark 4.

Pound the ginger, garlic and chillies into a coarse paste with a little water.

Heat the oil in a saucepan and fry the onions until they are golden brown. Set some aside for a garnish. Drain the lentils and add them to the onions with a little salt and the chilli paste. Fry for a few seconds, then add the lamb. Stir for a minute or two, then pour in the yogurt and take the pan off the heat.

Grease a deep ovenproof casserole with a lid. Place a layer of meat on the bottom of the dish. Cover it with a layer of the cooked rice and add 1 tablespoon of the melted butter, 2 teaspoons of the lemon juice and 2 teaspoons of the saffron strands with the milk. Repeat until all the ingredients have been used up ending with a layer of rice. Cover the dish, put it into the oven and bake for about 20 minutes. Do not open the dish until you are ready to serve, with Raita (see page 123) or Mixed Vegetable Curry (see page 60).

**Tip**
- Substitute beef rump steak for the lamb.

# Pork Vindaloo पोर्क विन्डालू

Vindaloo dishes appear on menus in Indian restaurants worldwide. This one is a kind of Portuguese pork stew seasoned with garlic and wine. Traditionally a vindaloo is made with pork, although pork is rarely eaten in India.

| Serves 3–4 | Preparation: 8 minutes | Cooking: 23 minutes |
| --- | --- | --- |

| | |
| --- | --- |
| 2 tbsp cider vinegar | 1 tsp cumin seeds |
| ¼ tsp salt | ½ tsp ground cinnamon |
| 500 g / 1 lb 2 oz casserole pork, trimmed and cubed | ¼ tsp ground cloves |
| | ½ tsp paprika |
| 8 dried red chillies | 3 tbsp groundnut oil |
| 3 garlic cloves, peeled and crushed | 1 onion, peeled and chopped |
| 2 tsp peeled and grated root ginger | |

Pour the cider vinegar into a bowl and dissolve the salt in it. Then add the pork and leave it to soak.

Meanwhile, put into the blender the chillies, garlic, ginger, cumin, cinnamon, cloves, paprika and 1 tablespoon of the oil and whiz to a paste.

Heat the remaining oil in a frying pan and sauté the onions until they are golden brown. Tip in the pork with the vinegar – carefully, it will hiss and perhaps spit – and brown it. Then add the spicy paste and stir thoroughly for a couple of minutes. Pour in 125 ml/5 fl oz just-boiled water, stir again, then cover and simmer for 15 minutes, or until the pork is thoroughly cooked. Serve with basmati rice or crusty rustic bread.

**Tip**
- Use ½ teaspoon of chilli powder if you have no dried red chillies.

# Seasoned Pork Chops

Masaledaar Pork Chop मसालेदार पोर्क चोप

Many Indian pork recipes come from Goa where the Portuguese left their mark on native cooking. Garlic and pork make a great team and chops are so quick to cook. They can also be grilled or pan-fried.

| Serves 2 | Preparation: 5 minutes | Cooking: 23 minutes |
| --- | --- | --- |

| | |
| --- | --- |
| 2 tsp curry paste *or* powder | Pinch of salt |
| 2 cloves garlic, peeled and crushed | 2 pork chops |
| 2 tsp peeled and grated root ginger (optional) | |

Mix together the curry paste or powder, the garlic, ginger (if using) and the salt, then smear this paste over the chops. Cook them under a medium grill for 20 minutes, turning occasionally. Serve with jacket potatoes and green beans.

**Tip**
- Before cooking the chops, make cuts in the outer edges of the fat on each chop so that they don't curl during cooking.

# Meatballs in Tomato and Chilli Sauce

Mirch Mutton Kofta मिर्च मटण कोफ्ता

My friend Werner, from Gouda in Holland, has always been used to simple food but he loved this hot, spicy sausage curry. It takes a little longer to prepare than some other dishes but if you have the time it's well worth the effort.

| Serves 3–4 | Preparation: 12 minutes  Makes 16–18 meatballs |
|---|---|
| | Cooking: 30 minutes |

| | |
|---|---|
| *For the Meatballs* | 2 cloves garlic, peeled and crushed |
| 2 green chillies, seeded and finely chopped | 1 green chilli, seeded and finely chopped |
| 2 cloves garlic, peeled and crushed | ½ tsp paprika |
| 2 tsp peeled and grated root ginger | ½ tsp ground cumin |
| 1 tbsp cornflour | ¼ tsp ground coriander |
| Juice of ½ lemon | ¼ tsp turmeric |
| ¼ tsp coarsely ground black pepper | ¼ tsp salt |
| 500 g / 1 lb 2 oz sausagemeat | 1 tsp lemon juice |
| *For the Tomato and Chilli Sauce* | 200 g / 7 oz can chopped tomatoes |
| 2 tbsp oil | ¼ tsp garam masala |
| 1 onion, peeled and chopped | |

First make the meatballs. Put into the blender the chillies, garlic, ginger, cornflour, lemon juice, black pepper and 2 tablespoons of water, then whiz to a paste. Mix it with the sausagemeat, then roll it into golf balls.

Now make the sauce. Heat the oil in a large saucepan or deep frying pan and fry the onion for 7–8 minutes, until golden brown. Then add the garlic, green chilli, paprika, cumin, coriander, turmeric, salt, lemon juice and tomatoes, and stir for 4 minutes. It should turn into a thick, dark red sauce. Now put the meatballs into the sauce and stir in 125 ml / 5 fl oz water. Leave it to cook for 6 minutes. Then stir in another 125 ml / 5 fl oz water, and cook for another 6–7 minutes. Take the pan off the heat, sprinkle over the garam masala, and serve with basmati rice.

**Tips**
- To speed up the cooking, shallow fry the meatballs in 4 tablespoons of oil for 5 minutes, then put them into the sauce for 6–7 minutes.
- If you have no sausagemeat, skin a few sausages.
- Substitute minced lamb for sausagemeat.

# Sausagemeat Shammi Kebabs
Mutton Shammi Kebab मटण शम्मी कबाब

Serve these as party snacks or you could use the mixture as a spicy stuffing for roast chicken.

| Serves 3–4 | Preparation: 10 minutes<br>Cooking: 10 minutes | Makes 16–18 patties |
|---|---|---|

| | |
|---|---|
| 400 g / 14 oz sausagemeat | 1 onion, peeled and very finely |
| ½ tsp chilli powder | chopped |
| 2 cloves garlic, peeled and | Juice of ½ lemon |
| crushed | 25 g / 1 oz fresh coriander leaves, |
| ¼ tsp garam masala | washed and chopped |

Preheat the oven to 180°C / 350°F / Gas Mark 4.

Mix together all the ingredients in a bowl. Form the paste into golf balls then flatten them. Lay them on a baking sheet and put them into the oven for 10 minutes.

Serve with tomato ketchup, Cumin Ketchup (see page 134) or Tomato and Chilli Chutney (see page 130).

**Tip**
- You can dry-fry the patties in a non-stick frying pan or grill them.

# Beef Madras Madras Beef मद्रास बीफ

Beef is not often eaten in India because practising Hindus regard the cow as a sacred animal. You could replace it with casserole lamb. The sauce with this dish is thick and fiery.

| Serves 2 | Preparation: 5 minutes<br>Cooking: 2 hours 15 minutes, plus 2 hours to marinade |
|---|---|

| | |
|---|---|
| 2 tsp curry paste *or* curry powder | 1 green chilli, seeded and chopped |
| 250 g / 8 oz lean diced casserole beef | ¼ tsp turmeric |
| 2 tbsp vegetable or groundnut oil | ¼ tsp salt |
| 1 onion, peeled and chopped | 1 tsp peeled and grated root ginger |
| 2 cloves garlic, peeled and sliced | |

Smear the curry paste or powder over the beef and leave it to marinate for at least 2 hours or overnight if possible.

Heat 1 tablespoon of the oil in a frying pan and sauté the meat for 5–6 minutes to brown the outside. Remove it from the pan and set it aside. Put the remaining oil into the pan and fry the onion, garlic and chilli for 8 minutes. Stir in the turmeric and salt. Then return the meat to the pan with 450 ml / 15 fl oz water. Cover and simmer over a low heat for 2 hours until the beef is tender. Stir in the ginger, and serve with plain basmati rice or naan bread (see page 115).

**Tip**
• Try adding 2 teaspoons of tomato purée with the water.

# Spam Masala स्पाम मसाला

I'm not a great fan of luncheon meat, but it does taste delicious when it is spiced up. It's a good stand-by too on a day when you're feeling broke but in need of a really tasty and comforting supper! And Richard Madeley, who is a member of the Spam Society (yes! it does exist!), loved this recipe.

| Serves 2 | Preparation: 5 minutes   Cooking: 7 minutes |
|---|---|

| | |
|---|---|
| 2 tbsp vegetable *or* olive oil | 1 tsp tomato purée |
| ½ onion, peeled and finely chopped | 1 tsp peeled and grated root ginger |
| 1 green chilli, seeded and chopped | 200 g / 7 oz can Spam or pork |
| 1 clove garlic, peeled and crushed | luncheon meat, cubed |

Heat the oil in a saucepan, then put in the onion and chilli and fry for 3 minutes until the mixture begins to turn golden brown. Add the garlic, tomato purée and ginger and stir for a minute. Then tip in the Spam and sauté for another minute. Add 65 ml / 3 fl oz water and cook until it has evaporated. Serve with hot pitta breads.

**Tip**
- If you're making Spam fritters, add ¼ teaspoon each of chilli and cumin powder to the batter.

# Vegetables
# ५ सब्जी

India has the largest number of vegetarians of any country in the world: millions of Hindus consider that it is wrong to kill animals for their flesh. In strict households neither fish nor eggs are permitted either. But countless different vegetables are available in India, which means that there are countless different ways to prepare them.

Indian vegetarian cuisine includes not just vegetables, but fruit, grains, nuts, pulses, herbs and spices. It is far from mundane or bland. You will find that one vegetable can be included in many different dishes to produce a variety of different flavours. Some are dry-fried with spices, without water, *bhujias*, and others are made into curries with sauce. Some vegetables, such as potatoes, are cooked before stir-frying, such as my Potatoes with Dried Red Chillies.

In Britain the selection of available vegetables is more limited but broaden your horizons by cooking with whatever you can find, and add a new dimension to your vegetables with a few spices. If you're unable to find fresh vegetables, spice up some frozen ones.

# Mixed Vegetable Curry

Mixed Sabzi Ki Curry मिक्स सब्जी की करी

Here is my simple and quick recipe for a mixed vegetable curry.

| Serves 2–4 | Preparation: 3 minutes   Cooking: 15 minutes |
| --- | --- |

2 tbsp oil

1 onion, peeled and chopped

1 green chilli, seeded and chopped

½ tsp ground coriander

½ tsp hot curry powder

400 g / 14 oz can chopped tomatoes

¼ tsp salt

350 g / 12 oz frozen mixed vegetables,
   defrosted

Heat the oil in a saucepan, then fry the onion and green chilli for 5 minutes until they have softened. Stir in the coriander and curry powder, then the tomatoes and salt. Continue to fry for another 30 seconds then add the mixed vegetables and cook for 2 minutes. Pour in 500 ml / 18 fl oz water, cover and simmer for 6 minutes. Serve with plain rice and a Tandoori Chicken with Coriander (see page 35).

## Tips

- Use a teaspoon of hot curry paste instead of the curry powder.
- Use fresh vegetables such as a mixture of carrots, cauliflower and green beans.

# Vege–Mince Curry
Shakahari Keema शाकाहारी कीमा

The brilliant thing about this product is that it is so quick to cook. Often it can only be bought ready-flavoured so I've only used curry powder in this recipe.

| Serves 2 | Preparation: 5 minutes   Cooking: 10 minutes |
|---|---|

| | |
|---|---|
| 2 tbsp olive *or* vegetable oil | ½ tsp curry powder |
| ½ onion, peeled and chopped | ¼ tsp salt |
| 1 clove garlic, peeled and crushed | 200 g / 7 oz Vege-Mince |
| 2 green chillies, seeded and chopped | 1 tsp peeled and grated root ginger |
| 1 tsp tomato purée | |

Heat the oil in a saucepan, then fry the onion, garlic and chillies for 2 minutes. Add the tomato purée, curry powder and salt, and stir-fry for 2 minutes. Then add the Vege-Mince and the ginger and continue to fry for another minute. Pour in 250 ml / 9 fl oz water and cook for 3 minutes. The finished dish should look quite dry. Serve with plain rice, pitta or chapatis (see page 117), and a tomato salad.

## Tips
- You can use any kind of meat-free mince produce, made from soya or Quorn.
- For a little colour, throw in some peas after you have fried the onions.

# Vegetable Korma Sabzi Korma सब्जी कोर्मा

In Indian restaurants korma dishes are known to be mild, and contain meat or vegetables cooked slowly with a small amount of liquid. After the main ingredient has been cooked, either nuts, yogurt, cream or butter is added to make the dish distinctively mild. I have added coconut to this one for its rich, aromatic flavour.

| Serves 2 | Preparation: 8 minutes   Cooking: 17 minutes |
|---|---|

| | |
|---|---|
| 1 tbsp vegetable oil | 50 g / 2 oz fine green beans, trimmed |
| 1 small onion, peeled and chopped | and chopped |
| ½ green chilli, seeded and chopped | 25 g / 1 oz peas, defrosted if frozen |
| 1 clove garlic, peeled and sliced | 3 tsp coconut powder or 2 tbsp |
| ¼ tsp ground cumin | coconut cream |
| Pinch of ground coriander | 1 tsp peeled and grated root ginger |
| ¼ tsp salt | Pinch of garam masala |
| 100 g / 4 oz carrots, peeled and sliced | |

Heat the oil in a saucepan, then add the onion, chilli and garlic and fry for 7 minutes until golden brown. Then put in the cumin, coriander and salt, and stir for a minute. Add all of the vegetables and cook for 2 minutes. Mix the coconut powder with 125 ml / 5 fl oz hot water from the kettle and add it to the pan, or stir in the coconut cream. Cover the pan and simmer over a very low heat for about 5 minutes or until the sauce is fairly thick. Add the ginger, then stir in the garam masala and take the pan off the heat. The sauce should be creamy yellow. Serve with chapatis (see page 117) or wholemeal pitta bread.

### Tips
- If you don't have any coconut, put in 1 tablespoon of cream or natural yogurt instead.
- Garnish with chopped almonds.

# Green Plantain Curry
Kele Ki Sabzi केले की सब्जी

Plantains are bananas that are only suitable for cooking. They are used frequently in south Indian dishes and my mother, who comes from western India, cooked with them in Mumbai. Surprisingly, they taste like potato so they are versatile and easy to cook.

| Serves 2–4 | Preparation: 5 minutes | Cooking: 14 minutes |
| --- | --- | --- |

| | |
| --- | --- |
| 2 green plantains | ¼ tsp turmeric |
| 1 tsp natural yogurt | ½ tsp ground coriander |
| 1 tbsp groundnut *or* vegetable oil | ¼ tsp salt |
| ¼ tsp cumin seeds | 1 tsp peeled and grated root ginger |
| ¼ tsp mustard seeds | 1 tbsp coconut powder *or* 2 tbsp |
| 1 green chilli, seeded and chopped | coconut cream |

With a vegetable peeler, remove a thin layer of the outer skin of the plantains, then cut them into slices around 2-cm / 1-in thick. Put them into a bowl and stir the yogurt into them with about 2 tablespoons of water. This will help to banish the stickiness. Leave them for a couple of minutes then wash and drain them.

Heat the oil in a saucepan, then put in the cumin and mustard seeds and fry for a couple of minutes. Add the plantains, chilli, turmeric, coriander, salt and ginger, stir for a minute, then pour in 125 ml / 5 fl oz water. Cover and simmer over a low heat for about 10 minutes. Stir in the coconut powder or cream, and cook for another minute. Serve with plain basmati rice, chapatis (see page 117) or pittas.

**Tip**
• Add 1 teaspoon of lemon juice at the end of cooking, if you like, for a sharper taste.

# Potatoes with Dried Red Chillies

Aloo Aur Lal Mirch Ki Sabzi

आलू और लाल मिर्च की सब्जी

When I first cooked this dish, I couldn't believe how easy it was to prepare – I still make it when I'm bored with mashed potato. My Dutch friend Werner cooks it regularly – he's crazy about mustard seeds.

| Serves 2–4 | Preparation: 15 minutes (if boiling potatoes)   Cooking: 10 minutes |
|---|---|

| | |
|---|---|
| 675 g / 1½ lb red-skinned potatoes, peeled | ½ tsp black mustard seeds |
| ¼ tsp salt | 4 pinches chilli powder *or* 4 dried red chillies |
| 4 tbsp sunflower *or* vegetable oil | ½ tsp turmeric |

Put the potatoes into a pan of boiling salted water, cover and cook for about 15 minutes until they are almost tender (or cook them in the microwave on high for 4 minutes). Drain them and set them aside until they are cool enough to handle, then quarter them so that they are all about the same size.

Heat the oil in a large frying pan. To check that it is at the right temperature, sprinkle in a few of the mustard seeds: if they pop, it is hot enough and you can add the remainder. Then add the chilli powder or the dried red chillies with the turmeric and salt. Fry for 1 minute, stirring continuously, until everything is well combined and aromatic. Then tip the potatoes into the pan and fry for about 4 minutes until they are smothered in seeds and the edges are crisp. Reduce the heat, cover the pan and cook for 5 minutes until the potatoes are tender. Serve at once as an accompaniment to a chicken or a meat curry.

### Tips
- Try substituting a fresh green chilli, finely chopped, for the dried chillies.
- Add 2 tablespoons of natural yogurt to the potatoes to take the heat out of the chilli.

p.64 | Potatoes with Dried Red Chillies

p.66 | Cabbage with Coconut and Dried Red Chilli

p.77 | Okra with Onions

p.83 | Salmon with Coriander and Red Onion

p.86 | King Prawn Masala

p.94 Baked Beans Balti

p.117 | Chapatis

p.118 | Deep-fried Breads (Pooris)

# Deep-Fried Potatoes in Curry Sauce
Dum Aloo दम आलू

*Dum* is an Indian method of steam-cooking food. The meat or vegetables are cooked first in a large amount of oil, ghee or butter, then covered and cooked over a very low heat for 30–60 minutes. My method for making this curry doesn't include steaming but the result is just as good. It's a robust curry with a velvety smooth sauce, and not an onion or tomato in sight. It comes from Kashmir.

| Serves 2–3 | Preparation: 12 minutes, including boiling time<br>Cooking: 11 minutes |
| --- | --- |

300 g / 10 oz baby salad potatoes

3 tbsp vegetable oil

¼ tsp salt

½ tsp garam masala

½ tsp chilli powder

¼ tsp fennel seeds (optional)

2 tbsp natural yogurt

½ tsp peeled and grated root ginger

25 g / 1 oz fresh coriander leaves, to garnish

Parboil the potatoes for 7 minutes, then drain them. Leave them to cool then peel and halve them. Prick them with a fork.

In a frying pan heat the oil, and sauté the potatoes for 3 minutes. Be careful – the oil may spit. Remove the potatoes from the pan with a slotted spoon and set them aside. In the same pan, add to the oil the salt, garam masala, chilli powder and fennel seeds, and mix. Return the potatoes to the pan with the spices, then tip in the yogurt and the ginger. Mix thoroughly for 2 minutes. The potatoes should look yellow with a thick sauce. Garnish with a few coriander leaves and serve with Mumbai Hot Lamb Curry (see page 48) or Jubilee Curry (see page 29) and rice.

**Tip**
• Add ½ teaspoon of sugar instead of fennel seeds.

# Cabbage with Coconut and Dried Red Chilli

Nariyal Aur Sukki Mirch Patta Gobi

नारियल और सूखी मिर्च पत्तागोभी

This is a variation on a south Indian dish which my friend Lopa, who's passionate about vegetarian cooking, loves. If you can get hold of some curry leaves, they're fantastic so add a few with the mustard seeds. Many friends who've never liked cabbage say that this recipe has converted them.

| Serves 2–4 | Preparation: 5 minutes   Cooking: 10 minutes |
|---|---|

| | |
|---|---|
| 4 tbsp groundnut or vegetable oil | ¼ tsp turmeric |
| ½ tsp brown mustard seeds | ¼ tsp salt |
| 2–3 dried red chillies | 15 g / ½ oz freshly grated or |
| 1 onion, peeled and thinly sliced | desiccated coconut |
| 200 g / 7 oz white cabbage, finely shredded | 2 tbsp lemon juice |

Heat the oil in a pan and carefully tip in the mustard seeds. Once they begin to pop, add the chillies then the onions, and fry for 2 minutes. Put in the cabbage, stir, and continue to fry for another 2 minutes. Add the turmeric and the salt. The cabbage will start to look bright yellow. Finally sprinkle over the coconut and the lemon juice and mix thoroughly. Take the pan off the heat, and serve with hot pittas or chapatis (see page 117) and Spicy Red Lentils (see page 96) or Pork Vindaloo (see pages 52–3).

### Tip
• If you cannot get hold of brown mustard seeds, use white ones.

# Tofu with Red Chilli

Lal Mirch Tofu लाल मिच टोफू

My friend Sudha is a staunch vegetarian and always keen to try new and exciting ways with tofu. I devised this recipe with her in mind. It's great as a snack with crusty bread.

| Serves 2–4 | Preparation: 5 minutes<br>Cooking: 15 minutes (includes 5 minutes' frying time) |
| --- | --- |

| | |
| --- | --- |
| 250 g / 8 oz tofu | ½ tsp ground cumin |
| 9 tbsp olive oil | ¼ tsp ground coriander |
| 1 medium onion, peeled and finely chopped | ¼ tsp salt |
| | 2 tsp tomato purée |
| 2 cloves garlic, peeled and sliced *or* crushed | 2 tbsp double cream |
| | 1 tsp peeled and grated root ginger |
| 1 red chilli, seeded and finely chopped | Couple of pinches of garam masala |
| ¼ tsp turmeric | |

Drain the tofu on kitchen paper and cut it into 1-cm / ½-inch cubes.

In a frying pan heat 6 tablespoons of the oil. Carefully place the tofu pieces in the pan and sauté for 5 minutes until golden brown – it may take longer. Drain it on kitchen paper and set to one side.

In a separate pan, heat the remaining oil and fry the onion for a couple of minutes. Then tip in the garlic and chilli and continue to fry until the mixture has browned, but don't let it burn. Then add the turmeric followed by the cumin, coriander and salt, stir-fry for a minute, then add the tomato purée. Then put in the tofu. Stir in 125 ml / 5 fl oz just-boiled water. In a small bowl, carefully mix the cream with 4 teaspoons of hot water. Pour the cream mixture slowly into the saucepan, then add the ginger, and heat gently. Don't let it boil or the mixture may curdle. Take it off the heat. Finally, sprinkle over the garam masala, and serve immediately with pitta bread and fresh green salad.

# Dry Cauliflower and Potato
Bhuni Aloo Gobi भुनी आलू गोभी

This dish comes from northern India where it is often served with a lentil dish. The cumin seeds liven up what is sometimes considered a dull vegetable – and certainly makes a change from cauliflower cheese!

| Serves 2 | Preparation: 10 minutes   Cooking: 19 minutes |
| --- | --- |

| | |
| --- | --- |
| 3 tbsp vegetable *or* olive oil | 200 g / 7 oz cauliflower florets |
| ½ tsp cumin seeds | ¼ tsp turmeric |
| 1 onion, peeled and chopped | ½ tsp ground coriander |
| 1 potato, peeled and diced | ¼ tsp salt |
| 1 green chilli, seeded and finely chopped | 1 fresh tomato, chopped |

Heat the oil in a saucepan, tip in the cumin seeds and fry for a few seconds. Then add the onion, potato and chilli and continue to cook for 5 minutes. Put in the cauliflower and stir-fry for 30 seconds. Stir in the turmeric, coriander and salt. Cover and cook over a low heat for 5 minutes. Add the tomato and mix well, cover, and cook for another 3 minutes. Serve with white pitta breads and Raita (see page 123).

**Tip**
- When using fresh cauliflower florets soak them in salted water for 5 minutes before cooking to encourage any resident caterpillars to leave. Then rinse.

# Butter Spinach Makhani Saag मखनी साग

My friend Naomi hates spinach – except when it's cooked like this. Asians love spinach but the variety found in India is different from the British kind. I sometimes use finely chopped frozen spinach or even the tinned variety. If you're using fresh leaves, make sure you wash them thoroughly, then blitz them in a food-processor or blender with a little water.

| Serves 2–4 | Preparation: 5 minutes | Cooking: 18 minutes |
| --- | --- | --- |

| | |
| --- | --- |
| 2 tbsp vegetable *or* olive oil | 1 tsp peeled and grated root ginger |
| 1 onion, peeled and chopped | ¼ tsp salt |
| 2 cloves garlic, peeled and chopped | 1 tsp tomato purée |
| 2 green chillies, seeded and finely chopped | 250 g / 8 oz can chopped spinach *or* finely chopped frozen spinach |
| ½ tsp turmeric | 25 g / 1 oz butter |
| ½ tsp ground cumin | 15 g / ½ oz fresh coriander leaves, washed and chopped |
| ¼ tsp ground coriander | |

Heat the oil in a saucepan and fry the onion, garlic and chillies for 6–7 minutes until the mixture is golden brown. Then add the turmeric, cumin, coriander, ginger, salt and tomato purée. Stir for a minute then tip in the spinach and the butter. Add 65 ml / 3 fl oz water and cook over a low–medium heat for about 8 minutes, stirring occasionally. Sprinkle over the coriander and serve with hot naan (see page 115) or as an accompaniment to Chicken Tikka Masala (see page 34) or Tarka Dal (see page 99).

### Tip
- When serving or reheating, add another knob of butter. It makes the spinach even creamier.

# Green Beans with Ginger and Mustard

Adrak Aur Rai Ki Hari Phulia

आद्रक और राय की हरी फलिया

Indian tradition has it that a mixture made from ginger – an aphrodisiac – honey and egg taken at night for a month is a remedy for impotence. I can't make the same claim for this dish, but it doesn't need much effort to cook and will impress any discriminating vegetarian.

| Serves 2 | Preparation: 3 minutes   Cooking: 7 minutes |
|----------|---------------------------------------------|

| | |
|---|---|
| 1 tbsp olive oil | 1 tsp ground cumin |
| ½ tsp mustard seeds | 1 tsp peeled and grated root ginger |
| 150 g / 6 oz green beans, trimmed and cut into 5-cm / 2-in pieces | ¼ tsp salt |

Heat the oil in a saucepan, then add the mustard seeds. A few seconds later, tip in the beans with the cumin and fry for 1 minute. Stir in the ginger and salt, and sauté over a low heat for 5 minutes. Serve hot with crusty ciabatta bread.

## Tips

- You can parboil the beans before sautéing them.
- Use ½ teaspoon nigella seeds instead of mustard seeds for a change.

# Masala Runner Beans
Masaledaar Phulia मसालेदार फलिया

An extremely quick dish to make with very little cooking involved.
The four spices spruce up the runner beans.

| Serves 2–4 | Preparation: 5 minutes   Cooking: 8 minutes |
|---|---|

| | |
|---|---|
| 2 tbsp vegetable or olive oil | 1 tsp ground cumin |
| 250 g / 8 oz runner or stringless flat | ¼ tsp chilli powder |
| beans, topped, tailed and sliced into | ¼ tsp turmeric |
| 2-cm / 1-in pieces | ¼ tsp ground coriander |
| ½ tsp peeled and grated root ginger | ¼ tsp salt |

Take a pan with a lid, heat the oil in it, then put in all the other
ingredients. Mix well, cover and simmer over a low heat for about
8 minutes until the beans are cooked. Serve with hot pitta bread, or
chapatis (see page 117) and Chicken Dhansak (see page 31).

**Tip**
- For a milder dish with more sauce fry one chopped onion in the oil for
  5 minutes, add the remaining ingredients, then add 125 ml / 5 fl oz water,
  and simmer for 8 minutes.

# Masala Mushy Peas Ragda Mattar रगड़ा मटर

Mushy peas are popular in Britain's chippies but I've gone a step further by seasoning them with a few simple spices. Marrowfat peas are not available in India, but many Indians stuff chapatis with mashed spiced fresh peas.

| Serves 2 | Preparation: 3 minutes   Cooking: 7 minutes |
|----------|---------------------------------------------|

1 tbsp vegetable oil

Knob of butter

1 onion, peeled and finely chopped

¼ tsp chilli powder

1 clove garlic, crushed

Pinch of asafoetida (optional)

Pinch of garam masala

¼ tsp ground cumin

¼ tsp ground coriander

300 g / 10 oz can marrowfat, or mushy, processed peas

Heat the oil in a frying pan and add the butter, onion, chilli powder, garlic and asafoetida. Fry the mixture for 5 minutes or until the onions are soft. Mix in the garam masala, cumin and coriander, cook for 30 seconds, then add the peas. Stir for a minute and serve with creamy mashed potatoes or on toast.

### Tip
- To sharpen the flavour, add a chopped tomato after you've fried the spices, and cook for 2 minutes before you add the peas.

# Green Peppers with Gram Flour
Besan Ki Simla Mirch बेसन की सिमला मिर्च

A delicious lunch snack eaten predominantly in the western parts of India, particularly Mumbai in Maharashtra.

| Serves 2–4 | Preparation: 3 minutes   Cooking: 10 minutes |
|---|---|
| 1 tbsp vegetable oil | ¼ tsp turmeric |
| ¼ tsp mustard seeds | ¼ tsp sugar |
| ¼ tsp cumin seeds | ¼ tsp salt |
| 3 medium green peppers, seeded and sliced | 4 tbsp gram (chickpea) flour |
| ¼ tsp chilli powder | 1 tsp chopped fresh coriander leaves (optional) |

Heat the oil in a frying pan, add the mustard and cumin seeds and fry for a few seconds until they pop. Then add the sliced peppers and continue frying for about 4 minutes. Sprinkle in the chilli powder, turmeric, sugar and salt and fry for a few more seconds. Mix in the gram flour spoonful by spoonful, and stir until it has browned, taking care not to let it burn at the bottom of the pan. Take it off the heat, scatter over the coriander leaves, and serve immediately with pitta bread, or as an accompaniment to Karahi Lamb (see page 50) or Butter Lentils (see page 95).

**Tips**
- The mustard seeds can be replaced with extra cumin seeds.
- To sharpen the flavour add 2 tablespoons of lemon juice.

# Roasted Aubergine
Baingan Bharta बेन्गन भरता

Roasted aubergine is a great summer dish, similar to the Greek aubergine dip. The aubergine originated in India but is now grown all over the world. Make sure you choose heavy ones: the light spongy ones contain lots of seeds.

| Serves 2–4 | Preparation: 10 minutes   Cooking: 10 minutes |
|---|---|

| | |
|---|---|
| 1 large aubergine | 1 tsp curry paste |
| 1 tbsp vegetable oil | ¼ tsp salt |
| 1 onion, peeled and finely chopped | 1 tsp tomato purée |
| 1 green chilli, seeded and chopped | 1 tsp lemon juice |

Skewer the aubergine on two forks and hold it over a naked flame, turning it, to blister the skin all over. Alternatively, preheat the oven to 180°C / 350°F / Gas Mark 4, and bake the aubergine for 10 minutes, or grill it until the skin turns brown. Then scoop the flesh into a bowl and mash or chop it. Heat the oil in a saucepan, add the onion and chilli and fry for 7 minutes until golden. Stir in the curry paste and salt with the tomato purée and cook for a minute. Tip in the aubergine and give it a good stir for a minute, then add the lemon juice.

Serve with pitta or toast or with crusty rolls.

### Tips
- Mash the aubergine to a purée and add 2 tablespoons of yogurt to make a dip.
- You can use tinned aubergines, which are available in Asian grocery stores.
- Instead of roasting the aubergine, you could chop it then boil it for 5 minutes until it softens. No need to skin it.

# Sugar-Snap Peas with Cumin and Ginger

Adrak Aur Jeera Ki Hari Phulia

आद्रक और जीरा की हरी फलिया

A spicier way of eating your greens – effortless to cook too.

| Serves 2 | Preparation: 2 minutes   Cooking: 5 minutes |
|---|---|

1 tbsp vegetable oil

¼ tsp cumin seeds *or* ground cumin

¼ tsp coarsely ground black pepper

150 g / 6 oz sugar-snap peas, strings removed

¼ tsp salt

1 tsp peeled and grated root ginger

Heat the oil in a wok or saucepan, and add the cumin seeds and black pepper. Fry for a minute, then put in the peas, salt and ginger. Cover and simmer for 3 minutes. Serve with Salmon with Coriander and Red Onion (see page 83) and ciabatta bread.

**Tip**
- Try this with petits pois instead of sugar-snaps.

# Simple Okra with Black Pepper
Kali Mirch Bhindi काली मिर्च भिन्डी

An excellent dish with which to introduce someone to the delights of okra, which is packed with flavour, minerals and vitamins, and needs little seasoning.

| Serves 2 | Preparation: 4 minutes   Cooking: 7 minutes |
|----------|---------------------------------------------|

| | |
|---|---|
| 100 g / 4 oz okra | Pinch of coarsely ground black pepper |
| 1 tbsp vegetable *or* olive oil | ¼ tsp salt |

Wash the okra whole and dry it thoroughly. When completely dry, slice off the tops and cut the okra into little rounds.

Heat the oil in a frying pan and put in the okra with the black pepper and salt. Sauté for 5–7 minutes, stirring regularly to make sure the okra doesn't burn. Serve with chapatis (see page 117) and some Greek-style yogurt.

**Tip**
- Do not add water to okra: it'll turn slimy. If you want a little sauce, stir in a tablespoon of yogurt at the end of cooking.

# Okra with Onions Bhindi Pyaz भिन्डी प्याज

Of all the tropical veggies, Indians love okra best. A friend of mine, who was used to eating spicy okra in a curry sauce, was amazed to discover its real taste when he tried this recipe. Here the okra is shallow fried – a north Indian method – and becomes deliciously crisp.

| Serves 2 | Preparation: 7 minutes | Cooking: 10 minutes |
| --- | --- | --- |

| | |
| --- | --- |
| 150 g / 6 oz okra | Pinch of turmeric |
| 2 tbsp vegetable *or* olive oil | ¼ tsp ground cumin |
| 1 small onion, peeled and chopped | ¼ tsp ground coriander |
| 1 clove garlic, peeled and sliced | 1 tsp peeled and grated root ginger |
| 1 green chilli, seeded and chopped | 2 tbsp fresh coriander leaves, washed |
| ¼ tsp salt | and chopped (optional) |

Wash the okra whole, then dry them thoroughly. Slice off the tops, discard them, and cut the remainder at an angle into bite-size pieces. Heat the oil in a frying pan and sauté the onion, garlic and chilli for 1 minute. Then add the okra, salt, turmeric, cumin and coriander. Continue to sauté for 5–6 minutes. It may turn slightly gooey, but as you cook it will dry out again. Then stir in the ginger, cook for 30 seconds and turn off the heat. Sprinkle over the coriander leaves and serve with chapatis (see page 117) and a dollop of Greek-style yogurt.

**Tip**
• Never cover okra while cooking: it'll turn slimy.

# Fish
# ६ मच्छी

When you look at a British Indian menu, you may be surprised to notice that there is hardly any fish on offer – strange when three-quarters of India is surrounded by water. However, perhaps the reason for this is because many restaurants are run by northern Indians, whose cuisine mainly consists of meat and poultry dishes. But things are changing: more and more restaurants are serving food from south India, Bengal in the east and Goa and Bombay in the west, where seafood has always been important. The staple diet of Bengalis is fish and rice. Pomfret, a flat fish caught along the Bombay coast and similar to Dover sole and plaice, is particularly popular in India. It's served fried, grilled, stuffed or made into curries, and has its own unique flavour. Singhara, available in the north, is similar to herring. Many fish available in India are not found in Britain, but you can replace them with your favourites.

Fried fish is popular in India. In Europe fish is usually coated with a plain flour batter but in India the fish is enhanced with a mixture of spices, lemon juice and a gram-flour batter. Coconut has a natural affinity with fish, and I've included a recipe for scallops in a herb-laced coconut curry – this sauce goes very well with any white fish. I've used tinned tuna for a quick chilli dish and my spicy fishcakes taste equally good with baked beans or a crisp green salad.

# Fish Curry Machchi Curry मच्छी करी

Simple and quick to make, with influences from south India and Goa.

| Serves 2 | Preparation: 3 minutes   Cooking: 12 minutes |
|---|---|

| | |
|---|---|
| ¼ tsp salt | 2 cloves garlic, peeled and sliced |
| ¼ tsp turmeric | 250 g / 8 oz cod fillet, skinned and cut |
| ¼ tsp ground cumin | into 5-cm / 2-in pieces |
| 1 tsp chilli powder | 200 ml / 7 fl oz can coconut milk |
| 2 tbsp vegetable or groundnut oil | 25 g / 1 oz coriander leaves, to garnish |

Mix together the salt, turmeric, cumin and chilli powder with 1 tablespoon of water and set it aside.

Heat the oil in a saucepan, then put in the garlic and brown it lightly. Add the fish and sauté carefully for 2 minutes. Stir in the spices and cook for another minute. Then pour in the coconut milk, cover and simmer for 3 minutes. Turn off the heat – the dish should be a lovely golden yellow with lots of sauce – and scatter over the coriander leaves. Serve with plain basmati rice and Butter Spinach (see page 69) or Masala Runner Beans (see page 71).

**Tips**
- If you think this dish may be too hot for you, use only ¼ teaspoon chilli powder.
- Substitute prawns for the cod.

# Sole Curry Sole Machchi Curry सोल मच्छी करी

Dover sole's size and bone structure is similar to that of pomfret, the white-fleshed non-oily fish found along the Mumbai coastline and used in this dish. However, it is so expensive that I suggest you use lemon sole or any of the alternatives listed below – unless you're feeling flush, of course!

| Serves 2–4 | Preparation: 5 minutes   Cooking: 8 minutes |
| --- | --- |

¼ tsp salt

½ tsp turmeric

¼ tsp chilli powder

4 × 300 g / 10 oz fillets lemon sole *or*
    haddock *or* monkfish, skinned

1 tbsp vegetable oil

2 cloves garlic, peeled and crushed

¼ tsp tamarind, sieved and seeded

¼ tsp ground cumin

¼ tsp ground coriander

1 tsp peeled and grated root ginger

Mix together the salt, turmeric and chilli powder, then rub it over the fish. Set aside for 5 minutes.

Heat the oil in a large saucepan and put in the garlic. Stir it around for a few seconds, then add the fish. Mix the tamarind with a little water, then stir in the cumin and coriander. Add 125 ml / 5 fl oz water, stir, and pour this spicy mixture over the fish. Cover and simmer over a low heat for 2 minutes, then add the ginger and stir. Continue to cook for another 3 minutes, then turn off the heat. The sauce will be a rich golden yellow. Serve hot with plain basmati rice.

## Tips
- For a milder dish, add 65 ml / 3 fl oz coconut milk.
- Add a fresh green chilli, seeded and chopped, instead of the chilli powder.
- Try halibut instead of sole, haddock or monkfish.

# Scallops in Coconut Curry
Nariyal Ki Scallop Curry नारियल की स्कोलप करी

Scallops are not generally found in India. However, like most seafood they taste wonderful with spices.

| Serves 2 | Preparation: 6 minutes   Cooking: 8 minutes |
|---|---|

2 tbsp coconut powder *or* 4 tbsp cream
2 tbsp Red Chilli Paste (see page 8)
1 tbsp vegetable oil

100 g / 4 oz scallops, with the coral,
  the ridge of muscle at the side,
  removed
25 g / 1 oz fresh coriander leaves

Mix the coconut powder with the Red Chilli Paste and 65 ml / 3 fl oz water. Take a saucepan with a lid, put in the oil and heat it. Add the Red Chilli Paste mixture and stir. Cover and simmer over a low heat for 6 minutes. Drop in the scallops, replace the lid and simmer for 2 minutes. Take the pan off the heat, scatter over the coriander leaves and serve with some nice crusty Italian bread, or plain basmati rice.

**Tip**
• Substitute prawns for the scallops.

# Salmon with Coriander and Red Onion

Hara Dhania Aur Pyaz Ki Machchi

हरा धनिया और प्याज की मच्छी

Here, the red onion and coriander complement the delicate flavour of the salmon. A speedy, exotic lunchtime offering.

| Serves 4 | Preparation: 5 minutes   Cooking: 10–12 minutes |
|----------|--------------------------------------------------|

4 fresh salmon steaks

50 g / 2 oz butter, melted

¼ tsp salt

1 tsp black pepper

1 red onion, peeled and chopped

1 Thai red chilli, seeded and chopped

50 g / 2 oz fresh coriander leaves,
   washed and coarsely chopped

2 cloves garlic, peeled and crushed

Brush the salmon steaks with some of the melted butter, then sprinkle with salt and black pepper. Place under a preheated moderate grill for 10–12 minutes, turning the steaks occasionally. Alternatively, cover the steaks with foil and place in the oven, preheated to 180°C / 350°F / Gas Mark 4, for 15 minutes.

Meanwhile, heat the remaining butter in a frying pan, add the onion and chilli and fry for 2 minutes. Stir in the coriander leaves and garlic, cook for another minute, then remove the pan from the heat. Serve the salmon steaks with the coriander and onion mixture, and a crisp rocket salad, or Sugar-Snap Peas with Cumin and Ginger (see page 75).

### Tip

- Make a sauce to go with the salmon: add a teaspoon of mild curry paste with 6 tablespoons of water to the onion and chilli mixture after frying and cook for 2 minutes. Pour over the steaks and serve.

# Fried Fish Masala
Talli Hui Masala Machchi तल्ली हुई मसाला मच्छी

In India, fish is fried in spiced gram flour batter, but in this recipe I have suggested marinating it in a simple blend of ground spices, which you should have in your store cupboard.

| Serves 2 | Preparation: 15 minutes   Cooking: 5 minutes |
|---|---|

350 g / 12 oz cod fillets, skinned and
   cubed
4 tbsp lemon juice
½ tsp salt
¼ tsp chilli powder

¼ tsp turmeric
¼ tsp ground coriander
½ tsp ground cumin
6 tbsp vegetable oil

Place the fish in a bowl and sprinkle over it the lemon juice. Blend or mix together the salt, chilli powder, turmeric, coriander, cumin and 3 tablespoons of oil. Smother the fish with the spiced oil and leave it to marinate for 5 minutes. Pour the remaining oil into a deep frying-pan and heat it. Put in the fish and cook for 2½ minutes, then turn it and cook for another 2½ minutes. Serve immediately with a crisp green salad.

**Tip**
- Instead of frying the fish, grill it on a piece of foil for 3 minutes on each side.

# Tuna Masala टुना मसाला

Tuna is not widely available in India so you will not find many Indian curry recipes that contain it. However, it needs little seasoning and this is a delicious and healthy snack.

| Serves 2 | Preparation: 5 minutes   Cooking: 9 minutes |
|---|---|

| | |
|---|---|
| 1 tbsp vegetable oil | ¼ tsp turmeric |
| 1 onion, peeled and chopped | 1 tsp ground cumin |
| 1 green chilli, seeded and finely chopped | 1 tsp tomato purée |
| 2 cloves garlic, peeled and finely chopped | 200 g / 7 oz can tuna in brine, drained |

Heat the oil in a frying pan, then put in the onion and fry for 4 minutes. Add the chilli and garlic, and continue to fry for a minute. Sprinkle in the turmeric, cumin and tomato purée. Stir well, then add the tuna and cook for another minute. Serve on buttered toast or as a sandwich filling.

### Tip
- If you'd like some sauce with this add 125 ml / 5 fl oz hot water with an extra teaspoon of tomato purée after you have put the tuna into the pan, and let it bubble for a minute or two.

# King Prawn Masala

Bada Jhinga Masala बडा झींगा मसाला

I experimented with a few ideas that came to me when I was looking at an Indian takeaway menu. This is what I hit upon – and it was quicker than dialling and waiting for a delivery!

| Serves 2 | Preparation: 4 minutes   Cooking: 15 minutes |
|---|---|

| | |
|---|---|
| 2 tbsp vegetable oil | ¼ tsp chilli powder |
| 1 onion, peeled and finely chopped | 2 tsp tomato purée |
| 2 cloves garlic, peeled and crushed | 150 g / 6 oz king prawns, peeled |
| ¼ tsp salt | Pinch of garam masala |
| ¼ tsp turmeric | Fresh coriander leaves, washed and |
| ¼ tsp ground cumin | finely chopped |
| ¼ tsp ground coriander | |

Heat the oil in a frying pan, put in the onion and fry until it is golden brown or caramelized, which should take about 8 minutes. Then add the garlic, salt, turmeric, cumin, coriander, chilli powder and tomato purée and stir for 30 seconds. Tip in the prawns and stir for 2 minutes. Add 65 ml / 3 fl oz water and continue to cook for a minute. Take the pan off the heat, sprinkle over the garam masala and the coriander leaves, and serve hot with pitta bread, Yellow Split Pea Curry (see page 102) and Green Beans with Ginger and Mustard (see page 70).

### Tip
• Add a teaspoon of tamarind concentrate instead of the tomato purée.

# Prawn Piri Piri Jhingha Piri Piri झींगा पिरी पिरी

This is a dish influenced by the cuisines of Goa and Portugal. When I was on holiday in Oporto, I enjoyed the local version. There, they use a large amount of paprika, and lots more oil and chilli than I have suggested here. Try it on a bed of lettuce.

| Serves 2 | Preparation: 5 minutes   Cooking: 7 minutes |
|----------|---------------------------------------------|

| | |
|---|---|
| 4 tbsp groundnut *or* vegetable oil | 200 g / 7 oz peeled prawns, defrosted if |
| 4 cloves garlic, peeled and crushed | frozen |
| 1 red chilli, seeded and finely chopped | ¼ tsp salt |

Heat the oil in a saucepan or wok, then put in the garlic and the chilli and fry for a minute. Add the prawns and the salt, and gently sizzle-fry for 5 minutes. Serve with crusty ciabatta for dipping into the sauce.

**Tip**
• If you haven't any fresh red chilli, add ¼ teaspoon of chilli powder.

# Prawns with Green Peppers

Jhinga Aur Simla Mirch झ्रीन्गा और शिम्ला मिर्च

The combination of green peppers and pink prawns makes this dish look irresistible. There's never any left over for the next day!

| Serves 2 | Preparation: 4 minutes   Cooking: 10 minutes |
| --- | --- |

2 tbsp vegetable oil

¼ tsp onion seeds (optional)

Pinch of asafoetida (optional)

¼ tsp turmeric

¼ tsp ground cumin

¼ tsp ground coriander

¼ tsp garam masala

¼ tsp salt

1 green pepper, seeded and sliced

2 green chillies, peeled and finely chopped

2 cloves garlic, peeled and crushed or sliced

2 tsp tomato purée

200 g / 7 oz prawns, cooked and peeled

Heat the oil in a frying pan until it is very hot, then add the onion seeds, if using, and fry them for a few seconds. Add the asafoetida, followed by the turmeric, cumin, coriander, garam masala and salt, and stir for a minute. Toss in the pepper, chillies and garlic and continue to fry for 3 minutes. Mix in the tomato purée, then fold in the prawns and allow them to sizzle in the pan for about 4 minutes. If you would like some sauce add 65 ml / 3 fl oz water. Take the pan off the heat and serve immediately with hot pitta bread.

### Tips
- No asafoetida? Use 1 sliced onion: add it just before you put in the pepper and fry it for a minute.
- If you haven't any fresh peppers use frozen chopped ones, defrosted.

# Fish Cakes Machchi Tikkiya मच्छी टिकिया

Indians from West Bengal cook fish cutlets in mustard oil, which gives them a sweet, nutty flavour. Here, I've suggested olive or vegetable oil, but you can use any oil that you like.

| Serves 2 | Preparation: 9 minutes | Cooking: 10 minutes |
|---|---|---|

| | |
|---|---|
| 200 g / 7 oz cod fillets, skinned | ¼ tsp ground cumin |
| ½ tsp vinegar | ¼ tsp chilli powder |
| ¼ tsp salt | 1 tbsp instant mashed potato powder |
| 1 clove garlic, peeled and crushed | 1 slice of dry toast, grated into crumbs |
| 1 tsp peeled and grated root ginger | 1 tbsp olive *or* vegetable oil |

Put the fish into the blender or food-processor with the vinegar, salt, garlic, ginger, cumin and chilli powder and whiz for 30 seconds. Make the mashed potato as directed on the packet, put it into a bowl, add the minced fish and mix thoroughly – it's easiest to do this with your hands. Divide the mixture into 4 equal portions, and shape each into a flat round (about 1 cm / ½ in thick). Cover the patties with the breadcrumbs. Heat the oil in a frying pan, then cook the fish cakes for 4 minutes on each side. Serve with tomato ketchup and fresh onion slices, or a crisp green salad.

### Tip
- Cook 1 peeled, diced potato in the microwave for 5 minutes then mash it instead of using instant mash.

# Pilchards in Tomato and Chilli Curry

Machli Tamatar Aur Mirch Ki Curry

मच्छली टमाटर और मिर्च की करी

When my mum and dad came to Britain in the sixties it was difficult to find Indian vegetables and other familiar ingredients, and there were few Indian restaurants. They were so desperate to adapt that they used whatever they could find to create something spicy, which is how this dish came about.

| Serves 2 | Preparation: 3 minutes   Cooking: 11 minutes |
|---|---|

| | |
|---|---|
| 1 tbsp vegetable oil | ¼ tsp ground coriander |
| 1 onion, peeled and finely chopped | ¼ tsp ground cumin |
| 2 cloves garlic, peeled and crushed *or* | ¼ tsp turmeric |
| sliced | 425 g / 14 oz can pilchards in tomato |
| ¼ tsp chilli powder | sauce |

Heat the oil in a frying pan and add the onion and garlic. Sauté for 5 minutes, or until the onion is golden brown. Add the chilli powder, coriander, cumin and turmeric. Stir well, then carefully tip in the pilchards with their sauce and cook for 5 minutes. Serve hot with chapatis (see page 117), pitta bread or plain basmati rice.

**Tip**
- If you fancy more sauce, add 125 ml / 5 fl oz water and let it bubble for a few minutes.

# Spiced Sardines Masala Sardine मसाला सारदीन

Sardines are an oily fish, packed with nutrients that may prevent heart disease and improve the skin. I try to eat at least one portion a week flavoured with a few of my favourite spices.

| Serves 2 | Preparation: 3 minutes   Cooking: 8 minutes |
| --- | --- |

1 × 125 g / 5 oz can of sardines in oil, spines removed

½ onion, peeled and chopped

2 cloves garlic, peeled and sliced

1 green chilli, seeded and finely chopped

1 tsp tomato purée

¼ tsp English mustard powder

¼ tsp ground cumin

Pour the oil from the can of sardines into a frying pan and heat it. Put in the onion and garlic and fry for a couple of minutes, then add the chilli and continue to fry for 4 minutes until the mixture browns. Stir in the tomato purée, the mustard powder and cumin. Add the sardines and let them warm through. Serve with Fresh Green Coriander Chutney (see page 125) and pitta bread or chapatis (see page 117).

**Tip**
• Use ½ teaspoon of made Dijon mustard if you haven't any English.

# Fried Mackerel

Talli Hui Bangda तल्ली हुई बान्गडा

Indians serve this snack with pre-dinner drinks. Eating mackerel with your fingers can be a bit fiddly and messy – although many happily fish out the odd bone missed – a bit like spare ribs. If you plan to serve this as a snack, have a few finger bowls ready with slices of lemon in the water for people to wash as my adventurous friend Patrick does. Otherwise serve it as a first course, with knives and forks!

| Serves 4 | Preparation: 5 minutes   Cooking: 8 minutes |
|---|---|
| 350 g / 12 oz mackerel fillets, skinned | ½ tsp turmeric |
| 1 tsp chilli powder | ¼ tsp mustard powder |
| 1½ tsp ground cumin | 1 tbsp rice flour |
| 1 tsp ground coriander | ½ tsp garlic purée |
| ½ tsp salt | 2–3 tbsp vegetable oil for frying |
| 1 tbsp malt vinegar | |

Slice the mackerel into pieces approximately 7 cm / 3 in long. Put them into a bowl and add all of the other ingredients except the oil and mix carefully.

Heat the oil in a frying pan, then put in the fish and fry for 8 minutes over a medium heat, turning them once. They will become crunchy and reddish-brown.

Serve with pitta bread and an onion salad. When you eat the mackerel, watch out for any little bones that might have been missed in the filleting process.

**Tips**
- Substitute plain flour for the rice flour if you need to.
- Substitute 1 clove of crushed fresh garlic for the garlic purée.

# Pulses and Dals
# ७ दाले

Dal, daal, dhal or dahl is the Hindi word for 'pulses'. Technically, the split pulses are dals, but many of us use the word to mean all pulses. India produces and consumes half of the world's pulses, and they are integral to almost every Indian meal.

Pulses are dried legumes, such as lentils, split peas and beans. Most lentil mixtures are served in restaurants as side dishes but they also make excellent meatless main courses – highly spiced, nutritious, packed with protein and delicious. As a side dish they will often balance the different flavours of a meal: for example, if the main course is spicy hot, a mildly seasoned dal will counteract the heat.

There are three popular ways of cooking dal: boil them and flavour them with butter and spices; soak then steam them with spices; cook them with vegetables, meat, fish or rice.

Although pulses often have to be cooked for ages, you can buy them tinned – they are just as good and save you the hassle of boiling them. Often, asafoetida and root ginger are added to pulse recipes to aid digestion. Red (masoor) and yellow (toor) lentils are thin and disc-shaped, quicker to cook and the easiest to digest.

If you don't have the particular dal I've suggested in the recipes that follow, replace it with another but do check the cooking times.

# Baked Beans Balti बेक बीन्ज बल्टी

A lot of British Asian families enjoy this as a quick lunchtime snack – it's a store-cupboard standby. Adapt the ingredients to suit what you have available.

| Serves 2 | Preparation: 2 minutes   Cooking: 8 minutes |
|---|---|

2 tbsp vegetable oil

1 onion, peeled and chopped

1 green chilli, seeded and finely chopped

¼ tsp garam masala

¼ tsp ground cumin

¼ tsp ground coriander

400 g / 14 oz can baked beans

Pinch of salt (optional)

Heat the oil in a small saucepan, then put in the onion. Fry for 1 minute, add the chilli and cook for a couple of minutes, stirring continuously, until the onion begins to turn golden brown. Add the spices and fry for another minute. Add the beans, reduce the heat and cook for 3 minutes. Taste, then season with salt, if necessary. Serve hot with chapatis (see page 117), naan (see page 115), pitta bread or toast.

### Tips
- You can substitute mushy peas for the beans.
- Stir in a knob of butter after you've added the beans for a creamier texture.

# Butter Lentils Dal Makhani दाल मखनी

Whenever we're on holiday anywhere in India my uncle Raj always orders this dish in restaurants. We've tried to persuade him to try something different but he's a bit of a stick-in-the-mud. I suppose he loves the rich creaminess – and who can blame him?

| Serves 2–4 | Preparation: 5 minutes | Cooking: 11 minutes |
| --- | --- | --- |

| | |
| --- | --- |
| 50 g / 2 oz butter | ¼ tsp chilli powder |
| 1 onion, peeled and chopped | ¼ tsp ground cumin |
| 2 cloves garlic, peeled and crushed | ¼ tsp ground coriander |
| Pinch of garam masala | 400 g / 14 oz can green lentils, drained |
| ¼ tsp salt | and washed |
| ¼ tsp turmeric | 1 tbsp double cream |

Heat the butter in a saucepan, put in the onions and garlic and fry for 6 minutes until the onions have browned. Add the garam masala, salt, turmeric, chilli powder, cumin and coriander and fry for a minute. Tip in the lentils, then add 125 ml / 5 fl oz water, and cook for 5 minutes. Take the pan off the heat, stir in the cream, and serve with pitta bread or as an accompaniment to Chicken Jalfrezi (see page 32).

**Tip**
- You can use any kind of dal for Dal Makhani, but be sure to cook them thoroughly.

# Spicy Red Lentils Masala Dal मसाला दाल

My friend Neely, a West London girl at heart, has just moved to Atlanta in America where Indian ingredients are hard to find. When she comes over to the UK she buys a six-month supply to take back with her. She misses good Indian food and says she could eat rice and lentils every day with some natural yogurt and a hot pickle.

| Serves 2–4 | Preparation: 4 minutes   Cooking: 16 minutes |
|---|---|

250 g / 8 oz red lentils

1 tbsp butter

1 onion, peeled and chopped

Pinch of turmeric

1 clove garlic, peeled and sliced

1 dried red chilli *or* 1 green chilli, stalk
  removed but left whole

¼ tsp salt

Soak the lentils in a bowl of cold water for about 3 minutes. Drain them. Take a saucepan with a lid, put in the butter and let it melt. Add the onion and fry for 5 minutes. Then put in the turmeric, garlic, chilli and salt and mix. Cook for a minute. Tip in the drained lentils and stir again. Then pour in 500 ml / 18 fl oz just-boiled water. Cover the pan and simmer for about 10 minutes or until the lentils are soft. Check half-way through to make sure that the water hasn't evaporated. If it looks dry, add a little more and continue to simmer. The finished dal will be thick and yellow.

Serve with plain basmati rice or brown pitta bread and Seasoned Pork Chops (see page 53).

### Tip
- If you make this ahead of when you want to eat it, add more butter or a tablespoon of yogurt when you reheat it.

# Green Lentils Hara Dal हरा दाल

Lentils are low in fat and high in protein and fibre. Green lentils have an earthy flavour that combines well with spices. However, if they are overcooked they turn mushy and lose their shape. Check the packet for the cooking time.

| Serves 4 | Preparation: 16 minutes |
|---|---|
| | Cooking: 10 minutes, plus 45 minutes for soaking and boiling the lentils |

| | |
|---|---|
| 250 g / 8 oz green lentils | ¼ tsp turmeric |
| 2 tbsp vegetable oil | Pinch of chilli powder |
| 1 onion, peeled and finely chopped | ¼ tsp ground cumin |
| 2 cloves garlic, peeled and chopped | ¼ tsp ground coriander |
| 1 green chilli, seeded and chopped | Generous knob of butter |
| ¼ tsp salt | Pinch of garam masala |

Soak the lentils in 500 ml / 18 fl oz just-boiled water for 30 minutes. Then drain and rinse them, put them into a saucepan with 625 ml / 23 fl oz just-boiled water and boil gently for 15 minutes until they have softened. Don't drain them.

Meanwhile heat the oil in a saucepan and fry the onions and garlic for 9 minutes, then add the chilli and fry for 20 seconds. Stir in the salt, turmeric, chilli powder, cumin and coriander and cook for a minute. Tip in the lentils with their water, stir, then add the butter and 125 ml / 5 fl oz water. Cook for 4 more minutes, and then take the pan off the heat and sprinkle over the garam masala. Serve with fluffy white rice or naan (see page 115).

**Tip**
- If you're in a hurry, use ready-cooked tinned green lentils.

# Skinned Split Black Lentils with Garlic

Lasooni Urad Dal लसूनी अ्रढ दाल

These lentils are rich, very creamy and delicious, but too heavy to eat every day. Buy a 500 g / 1 lb 2 oz packet from an Indian grocer – it will keep for about 4 months.

| Serves 2–4 | Preparation: 5 minutes, plus 1 hour to soak the lentils<br>Cooking: 10 minutes, plus 25 minutes to boil the lentils |
|---|---|

| | |
|---|---|
| 250 g / 8 oz skinned split black lentils | ½ tsp turmeric |
| 3 tbsp groundnut *or* vegetable oil | ¼ tsp salt |
| 1 medium onion, peeled and chopped | 1 tsp ground cumin |
| 3 cloves garlic, peeled and crushed or sliced | ¼ tsp garam masala |
| | 2 tsp tomato purée |
| 2 green chillies, seeded and chopped | 2 tsp peeled and grated root ginger |

Soak the lentils in water for 1 hour, then drain and rinse them. Put them into a saucepan with 250 ml / 8 fl oz water and boil gently for 25 minutes until they are soft. From time to time, remove and discard the scum that will form on the top. Don't drain them.

Meanwhile, heat the oil in a saucepan, put in the onion and fry for 1 minute, then add the garlic and chillies and continue to fry for 5 minutes or until the mixture begins to turn golden brown. Stir in the turmeric, salt, cumin and garam masala, stir for a minute, then the tomato purée and ginger, and stir again for 30 seconds. Add the boiled lentils with their water and cook for another minute. The lentils should be reddish yellow. Take the pan off the heat, and serve with hot buttered wholemeal pitta bread and an onion salad.

### Tips
- For a richer dish, mix in 2 tablespoons of butter just after you've added the lentils to the cooked spices.
- If you can't get hold of skinned split black lentils, use mung beans instead.

# Tarka Dal तडका दाल

'*Tarka*' or '*tadka*', which you may have seen on a restaurant menu, is not a variety of dal but the name of a process of cooking in which spiced butter is used to season a dish. It's a technique also used in flavouring vegetables and sometimes meat.

| Serves 2–4 | Preparation: 5 minutes |
|---|---|
| | Cooking: 13 minutes, plus 20 minutes to boil the lentils |

| | |
|---|---|
| 300 g / 9 oz yellow mung dal | 1 onion, peeled and chopped |
| ½ tsp turmeric | 2 cloves garlic, peeled and crushed |
| ¼ tsp ground coriander | ¼ tsp chilli powder |
| 30 g / 1 oz butter | ¼–½ tsp salt |
| ¼ tsp cumin seeds | ½ tsp garam masala |
| Pinch of asafoetida | Fresh coriander leaves |

Wash and drain the dal, then boil it in 850 ml / 30 fl oz of water with the turmeric and ground coriander for 15–20 minutes until it is frothy and soft. In a wok or frying pan, melt the butter and put in the cumin seeds with the asafoetida, stir them around, then add the onion and garlic and fry for 6 minutes. Sprinkle in the chilli powder and salt, then tip in the cooked dal and fry for another 5 minutes. Then stir in the garam masala. Add 125 ml / 5 fl oz water if the consistency seems too thick. Take the pan off the heat, scatter over the coriander leaves and serve with hot chapatis (see page 117) or pitta bread.

### Tip
- When reheating the dal, add a knob of butter.

# Chickpea Salad Chana Salad चना सलाद

This has a lovely nutty flavour. It makes an excellent side dish with Tandoori Chicken (see page 35).

| Serves 2–4 | Preparation: 4 minutes   Cooking: 4 minutes |
|---|---|

1 tsp olive oil

¼ tsp cumin seeds

¼ tsp mustard seeds

1 onion, peeled and sliced

1 × 400 g / 14 oz can chickpeas,
   drained and rinsed

¼ tsp salt

1 tbsp lemon juice

1 tbsp desiccated coconut

25 g / 1 oz fresh coriander leaves

Heat the oil in a saucepan and put in the cumin and mustard seeds. Fry the spices until they pop, then add the onion and stir for 2 minutes. Add the chickpeas and salt then turn off the heat. Pour in the lemon juice and the desiccated coconut, and mix well. Tip the salad into a bowl, garnish with a few coriander leaves and serve with Tandoori Chicken or Karahi Lamb (see page 50) or Lamb Kebabs (see page 138).

### Tips
- Drizzle 1 teaspoon of sesame oil over the chickpeas just before serving.
- Add 1 finely chopped red chilli after you have put in the salt.

# Chickpea Curry Chana Masala चना मसाला

| Serves 2 | Preparation: 3 minutes | Cooking: 19–20 minutes |
|---|---|---|

| | |
|---|---|
| 1 tbsp groundnut oil *or* butter | ¼ tsp chilli powder |
| 1 onion, peeled and chopped | 2 fresh tomatoes, chopped, *or* 1 x 200 g / |
| 1 clove garlic, peeled and crushed | 7 oz can tomatoes |
| ¼ tsp salt | 1 x 400 g / 14 oz can chickpeas, |
| ½ tsp ground cumin | drained and rinsed |
| ¼ tsp ground coriander | 1 tsp peeled and grated root ginger |
| ¼ tsp turmeric | Pinch of garam masala |

Heat the oil in a deep saucepan or a medium wok then put in the onion and garlic. Fry for 8–9 minutes until the onions have caramelized. Then add the salt, cumin, coriander, turmeric and chilli. Stir-fry for a minute then tip in the tomato, followed by the chickpeas. Continue to stir, crushing a few of the chickpeas as you do so. Pour in 125 ml / 5 fl oz water, then cover and simmer for 5 minutes. At this point, stir in the ginger and garam masala, cook for another minute, then turn off the heat. Serve spooned over Lattice Potato Cakes (see page 16) with some natural yogurt.

### Tip

- If you're using dried chickpeas soak them overnight, then boil them for at least half an hour, until they're cooked.

# Yellow Split Pea Curry

Peeli Mattar Dal पीली मटर दाल

Split peas are available in supermarkets and from Asian food shops. They are used in many different street snacks, and are also folded into bread doughs. Chapatis sometimes contain split peas.

| Serves 2–4 | Preparation: 5 minutes, plus 8 hours' soaking time and 1 hour boiling time    Cooking: 15 minutes |
|---|---|

| | |
|---|---|
| 250 g / 8 oz yellow split peas | 1 garlic clove, peeled and sliced |
| 2 tbsp groundnut oil | 1 tsp curry powder |
| 1 onion, peeled and chopped | ¼ tsp salt |
| 1 green chilli, seeded and chopped | |

Soak and cook the split peas as instructed on the packet. Don't drain them after cooking. In a saucepan, heat the oil then add the onion, chilli and garlic and fry for 7–8 minutes, until golden brown. Stir in the curry powder, the salt and the split peas with their water. If the split peas begin to stick to the bottom of the pan, add 125 ml / 5 fl oz more water and cook for 2 minutes. Serve with plain basmati rice.

### Tips
- Add a pinch of asafoetida when frying the onions.
- Soak the split peas in water hot from the kettle to speed up the softening process.

# Kidney Bean Curry Rajma Curry राजमा करी

Kidney beans are used commonly in northern Indian cooking. On the meandering mountainous routes from Jammu to Kashmir, countless little restaurant shacks sell them to eat with rice – *rajma* with *chawal* – and a hot spiced tea.

| Serves 2 | Preparation: 3 minutes   Cooking: 15 minutes |
|---|---|

| | |
|---|---|
| 2 tbsp olive *or* vegetable oil | ¼ tsp salt |
| 1 medium onion, peeled and chopped | ¼ tsp garam masala |
| 2 cloves garlic, peeled and sliced *or* crushed | 1 tsp peeled and grated root ginger |
| 1 green chilli, seeded and chopped | 1 tsp tomato purée |
| ¼ tsp turmeric | 1 × 400 g / 14 oz can kidney beans, washed and drained |
| ¼ tsp ground cumin | Knob of butter (optional) |
| ½ tsp ground coriander | |

Heat the oil in a saucepan then put in the onion and garlic. Fry for 5–6 minutes, then add the chilli. Stir in the turmeric, cumin and coriander followed by the salt and garam masala and cook for a minute. Add the ginger and fry for a minute, then stir in the tomato purée. Tip in the beans and mix them well into the spice mixture, continuing to fry for another minute. Now pour in 200 ml / 7 fl oz water, cover the pan and simmer over a very low heat for about 3 minutes until the curry thickens or the oil floats to the surface – pour it off, if you like. Stir in the butter, if you are using it, and serve with plain basmati rice.

## Tips
- If you're using dried kidney beans soak them overnight and boil them thoroughly the next day.
- Try adding a 200 g / 7 oz can of chopped tomatoes.
- If you don't have any garam masala, use 1 teaspoon of curry paste instead.

# Indian Bean Hotpot

Desi Daalon Ka Casserole देसी दालो का केसेरोल

I used a can of mixed pulses, containing kidney beans, black-eye beans, pinto beans and chickpeas, for this dish. It's protein-packed and makes a nice wintry alternative to a meat stew.

| Serves 2–4 | Preparation: 5 minutes | Cooking: 18 minutes |
|---|---|---|

50 g / 2 oz butter

1 onion, peeled and chopped

2 cloves garlic, peeled and sliced

1 tsp hot curry powder

1 × 200 g / 7 oz can chopped tomatoes

1 × 400 g / 14 oz can mixed pulses, washed and drained

1 tsp peeled and grated root ginger

Pinch of salt

25 g / 1 oz fresh coriander leaves, washed and chopped, for garnish

Melt the butter in a saucepan and put in the onions and garlic, then fry for 5 minutes until they turn golden. Add the curry powder and tomatoes, then cook over a high heat for 5 minutes until the butter surfaces on the top. The mixture should reduce to a thick dark red paste. Add the mixed pulses and the ginger, season with salt and stir well, mashing a few of the beans while you do so. Cook for 3 more minutes. Then pour in 125 ml / 5 fl oz hot water from the kettle and let the hotpot stew for another 5 minutes. Scatter over the coriander and serve with plain rice, pitta bread or a jacket potato, and a simple green salad.

### Tips
- Make the hotpot with a single pulse, such as kidney beans. If you use dried beans, make sure they're cooked thoroughly before you eat them.
- If you have time, add 275 ml / 9 fl oz water, cover and bake the casserole in an ovenproof dish at 160°C / 325°F / Gas Mark 3 for 1 hour.

# Curried Broad Beans
Phulion Ki Dal फलियो की दाल

Fresh broad beans are available in the spring and summer. The spices in this recipe complement their sweet flavour and earthy texture.

| Serves 4 | Preparation: 5 minutes | Cooking: 12 minutes |
| --- | --- | --- |

2 tbsp vegetable *or* groundnut oil

1 onion, peeled and chopped

1 clove garlic, peeled and chopped

1 tbsp curry powder *or* curry
   paste

¼ tsp salt

400 g / 14 oz frozen broad beans,
   defrosted

1 tsp lemon juice

1 tsp peeled and grated root ginger

25 g / 1 oz fresh coriander leaves

Heat the oil in a saucepan, then fry the onion and garlic for 5 minutes until they are golden. Stir in the curry powder or paste and salt, cook for a minute, then add the beans and stir-fry for 2 minutes. Pour in 125 ml / 5 fl oz hot water from the kettle, then cover and simmer for 4 minutes, stirring half-way through. Take the pan off the heat, mix in the lemon juice and ginger, then scatter over the coriander leaves. Serve with mashed potatoes, chapatis (see page 117) or pitta bread.

**Tip**
• Try this recipe with butter beans.

# Rice and Breads
# ८ चावल और रोटी

Many of my friends have said they find cooking rice difficult. But it needn't be, if you follow the instructions on the packet. I tend to rinse my rice under the cold tap until the water runs clear before I cook it. This gets rid of the starch that clings to the grains.

There are hundreds of varieties of rice, but the one principally associated with Indian cooking is basmati, a long-grain type grown along the foothills of the Himalayas. It is considered to be the best – and most expensive – rice in the world. Fluffy and less sticky than other varieties, it has a delicate flavour and a distinct nutty aroma when cooked.

In the south of India no meal is conceivable without rice, it is used not only as an accompaniment to a curry but for creating all sorts of dishes such as spiced pulaos and meaty biryanis. The grains can be soaked with lentils then ground to a thick batter, which is fermented and made into pancakes called *dosai*.

In Hindi *roti* means bread. From paper-thin pooris to puffed-up chapatis, most Indian breads are unleavened. They are a dietary staple, but are also used to scoop up meat and vegetables and mop up sauces. Most Indian breads are at their best when they're eaten hot within a few minutes of cooking. Many Indian households in Britain eat chapatis every day, but naan is more popular in restaurants. The basic naan is a wheatflour bread leavened with a starter such as yeast then baked in a *tandoor*. If you visit a restaurant with an open *tandoor*, or clay oven, you may be able to watch the cook shaping the balls of dough, then slapping them on to the side of the oven where they stick until they are done. The cook peels them off a split second before they fall.

The bread and rice divide separates the north from the south of India. Although rice is an important staple in the north, the breads stand out there.

# Basmati Rice Basmati Chawal बासमती चावल

This saves me all the hassle of draining off the water afterwards. My friend Naomi is still bewildered by how I can cook rice so quickly. I think the secret is not to touch the pan for 10 minutes.

Preparation: 3 minutes    Cooking: 10 minutes

| Rice | Water | Serves |
|---|---|---|
| 200g/7oz | 375ml/14 fl oz | 2 |
| 400g/14oz | 750ml/1¼ pints | 2–3 |
| 600g/1lb 4oz | 1125ml/2 pints | 3–4 |
| 800g/1lb 12oz | 1500ml/2¾ pints | 4–5 |

Rinse the rice under running cold water to remove as much of the starch as possible. Then put it into a saucepan with a dash of oil and a pinch of salt. Pour in the appropriate amount of boiling water and cover the pan with the lid. Simmer over a very low heat for about 10 minutes. You'll know when the rice is ready because most of the water will have disappeared. Check a few of the grains to see if they're cooked.

### Tips
- The oil you add before cooking helps to keep the grains separate.
- Always store any leftover cooked rice in a covered container in the refrigerator.
- When reheating cooked rice, always make sure it's very hot before you serve it.

# Pulao Rice Chawal Pulao चावल पुलाव

The pulao was created by the Indian Moghuls of the sixteenth century, who were inspired by Persian cooking. It's an elaborate dish, flavoured with whole spices and studded with meat and vegetables. I've prepared a plainer version.

| Serves 2 | Preparation: 3 minutes   Cooking: 18 minutes |
|---|---|

| | |
|---|---|
| 1 tbsp vegetable oil *or* 1 tbsp butter | ¼ tsp cumin seeds |
| 2 green cardamoms | 1 small onion, peeled and thinly sliced |
| 2 cloves | 200 g / 7 oz basmati rice |
| 2.5 cm / 1 in piece cassia bark *or* cinnamon | ¼ tsp salt |

Heat the oil or butter in a pan with a lid. Put in the cardamoms, cloves, cassia bark or cinnamon, and cumin seeds. Stir for a second or two, then add the onion and fry for 5 minutes until soft. Then tip in the rice, add the salt and stir for 30 seconds. Add 500 ml / 18 fl oz boiled water from the kettle, cover the pan and simmer over a low heat for 8 minutes until the rice is cooked. Try not to lift the lid of the pan while the rice is cooking. Serve with any chicken or fish dish.

### Tips
- For a bit of colour, add a pinch of turmeric when you add the rice to the spices.
- If the butter turns brown or burns while you're heating it in the pan, throw it away and start again.

# Vegetable Pulao

Sabziyon Ka Pulao सब्जियो का पुलाव

Rice absorbs the flavours of any ingredient that you throw in with it so Indians make all kinds of sweet and savoury dishes with it. This vegetable pulao is served on special occasions and at dinner parties.

| Serves 2–4 | Preparation: 3 minutes | Cooking: 20 minutes |
| --- | --- | --- |

2 tbsp vegetable oil

1 black cardamom (optional)

1 green cardamom

2.5 cm / 1 in piece cassia bark *or*
    cinnamon

2 cloves

2 black peppercorns

1 onion, peeled and sliced

300 g / 10 oz frozen mixed vegetables,
    defrosted

¼ tsp salt

¼ tsp ground cumin

300 g / 10 oz basmati rice, rinsed
    thoroughly

Heat the oil in a deep saucepan with a lid. Put in the black and green cardamoms, the cassia bark or cinnamon, the cloves and the peppercorns. Stir for a moment so that they release their fragrance. Then add the onion and fry them for about 4 minutes or until they turn a light brown. Do not let them caramelize. Tip in the vegetables and the salt and fry gently for 5 minutes. Now sprinkle in the cumin and add the rice. Stir everything well, and pour in 600 ml / 1 pint just-boiled water. Cover and simmer for 10 minutes, or until the rice has cooked.

Serve hot with Raita (see page 123).

### Tips
- Try this with different combinations of vegetables.
- Substitute drained tinned vegetables if you need to. However, fry them for less time because they will already have been cooked.

# Chicken Pulao Murg Pulao मुर्ग पुलाव

When I'm bored with curry, I turn to this dish, which is a meal in itself. You can use any part of the chicken – legs, thighs or breasts.

| Serves 4 | Preparation: 5 minutes   Cooking: 20 minutes |
|---|---|

2 tbsp vegetable *or* groundnut oil

4 green cardamoms

2 black cardamoms (optional)

¼ tsp cumin seeds

2 pieces cassia bark *or* cinnamon

2 dried red chillies

5 black peppercorns

2 cloves garlic, peeled and chopped

1 small onion, peeled and sliced

250 g / 8 oz chicken pieces, skinned
   and cut into bite-size pieces

1 tsp peeled and grated root ginger

½ tsp turmeric

Knob of butter

½ cup natural yogurt

½ tsp salt

Juice of ½ lemon

400 g / 14 oz basmati rice, rinsed
   thoroughly

¼ tsp garam masala

Heat the oil in a large saucepan or wok. Throw in the green and black cardamoms, cumin seeds, cassia bark or cinnamon, the chillies, peppercorns and garlic. Stir for 30 seconds, then tip in the onion. Fry this pungent mixture for 1 minute to release the flavours of all the spices. Add the chicken, ginger, turmeric and butter. Sauté the chicken for about 4 minutes, or until the chicken appears cooked on the outside. Stir in the yogurt, salt and lemon juice, then fold in the rice. Pour in 875 ml / 32 fl oz hot water and the garam masala, then cover and simmer over a low heat for 10 minutes until the rice is cooked. Serve with Raita (see page 123) and Mixed Vegetable Curry (see page 60).

**Tip**
- For a creamier, richer flavour, fry the spices in butter and use *crème fraîche* instead of yogurt.

# Tomato Rice Tamatar Chawal टमाटर चावल

This is the simplest of rice dishes, with few spices. The rice picks up the flavours of the tangy tomato and looks so vibrant.

| Serves 4 | Preparation: 3 minutes   Cooking: 13 minutes |
|---|---|

1 tbsp vegetable oil

1 clove garlic, peeled and crushed *or* chopped

400 g / 14 oz basmati rice (washed)

½ tsp salt

½ tsp ground cumin

200 g / 7 oz can chopped tomatoes

Heat the oil in a large saucepan with a lid, then fry the garlic for a few seconds. Carefully tip in the rice and stir for a minute. Add the salt, cumin and tomatoes, then pour in 750 ml / 27 fl oz boiling water. Cover and simmer over a low heat for about 10 minutes, or until the rice is cooked. It should have a lovely pink colour. Serve hot with Chicken Dhansak (see page 31) and Yogurt and Mint Raita (see page 123).

### Tip
- You can use a couple of fresh tomatoes instead of tinned ones, but you will need to add 1 litre / 35 fl oz water to the rice.

# Bacon Rice Bacon Chawal बेकन चावल

My mother used to cook this for my father, and for me when I was three years old. I loved bacon and rice, and when they were combined in one dish, I was in heaven!

| Serves 2 | Preparation: 3 minutes | Cooking: 15 minutes, 10 for cooking the rice |
|---|---|---|

1 tbsp olive *or* vegetable oil

2 rashers bacon, chopped

1 onion, peeled and chopped

1 clove garlic, peeled and sliced

¼ tsp ground cumin

Pinch of salt

200 g / 7 oz basmati rice, rinsed
  thoroughly

Heat the oil in a pan with a lid, then throw in the bacon and fry for a minute. Add the onions and garlic and fry for another minute, then add the cumin and salt. Fold in the rice, add 500 ml / 18 fl oz boiling water, cover and simmer for 10 minutes. Serve with Spicy Red Lentils (see page 96) or Vegetable Korma (see page 62) and Cucumber Raita (see page 123).

**Tip**
• For a little heat, add a pinch of garam masala with the cumin.

# Sweet Rice Mittha Chawal मीठा चावल

This dish is served at weddings and religious festivals, but it's so easy and quick to make that I often prepare it for a speedy snack.

| Serves 4 | Preparation: 5 minutes<br>Cooking: 5 minutes, plus 10 minutes for cooking the rice |
| --- | --- |

3–4 saffron strands

125 ml / 5 fl oz milk, warmed

50 g / 2 oz butter

4 whole cloves

2 green cardamoms, crushed

6 almonds, slightly crushed

8 pistachio nuts, slightly crushed

200 g / 7 oz basmati rice (dry weight), cooked

50 g / 2 oz sugar

Put the saffron in a bowl and pour over the warm milk. Leave it to stand. Heat a saucepan, put in the butter and when it has melted, add the cloves, cardamoms and nuts. Stir over the heat for a minute then tip in the cooked rice and continue to stir for 2 minutes. Carefully, a little at a time, mix in the sugar, then pour in the saffron milk and stir for another minute. Serve hot or cold.

### Tip
• If you want to remove the skins of the nuts, soak them in water first for about 10 minutes.

# Naan नान

These days you can buy naan in the supermarket, but why not make it fresh for a dinner party? Like most Indian breads, it is best eaten warm from the oven. Preparing Indian breads involves three processes: mixing, kneading and resting. This last stage is important in softening the dough and making it more elastic.

| Makes 4 naans | Preparation: 35–40 minutes | Cooking: 15 minutes |
|---|---|---|

| | |
|---|---|
| 1 tsp dried active yeast | ½ tsp baking powder |
| 1 tsp sugar | 1 tbsp vegetable oil |
| 200 g / 7 oz plain flour | 2 tablespoons natural yogurt |
| ¼ tsp salt | 2 tablespoons milk |

In a small bowl, mix the yeast with 1 tablespoon of warm water. Stir in the sugar and leave it in a warm place for 5 minutes until the yeast is covered with froth. Meanwhile mix together the flour, salt and baking powder then stir in the oil, yogurt and milk and lastly the yeast mixture. Knead the dough: clench your hand into a fist, wet the knuckles, then press them repeatedly into the dough. Continue pressing and kneading until you have a soft, pliable dough. It should take about 10 minutes. Place the dough in a mixing bowl, cover it with cling film and leave it in a warm place to rise for 10–15 minutes.

Preheat the oven to 140°C / 275°F / Gas Mark 1.

Divide the dough into 4 balls and, on a floured surface, roll each into a long oval shape about 0.5-cm / ¼-in thick. Don't roll them out too thinly or they'll turn out like crisps! Place them on a greased baking tray and put them into the centre of the oven for 10–15 minutes. They are ready when they have puffed up a little – they should be soft and crumbly, not chewy.

Serve with a chicken curry or a balti dish with mango chutney.

**Tip**
• Add a pinch of onion seeds for colour and spice.

# Peshwari Naan पेशवरी नान

Most naans are prepared in the *tandoor*, which looks like a large clay jar with an opening at the bottom for the fuel. *Tandoori* cooking originally came from the Middle East but is now popular all over the world.

| Serves 8 | Preparation: 8 minutes   Cooking: 15 minutes |
|---|---|

| | |
|---|---|
| 200 g / 7 oz self-raising flour | 5 tbsp water |
| 1 tbsp caster sugar | 1 tbsp sultanas |
| 1 tbsp ground almonds | ¼ cup single cream |
| 2 tbsp natural yogurt | |

Preheat the oven to 140°C / 275°F / Gas Mark 1. Put all of the ingredients into a large mixing bowl with 3 tablespoons of water, blend them together, then knead the dough (see page 115) for at least 4 minutes until it is soft and pliable. Divide it into 4 balls. Roll them out on a floured surface into a flat round or oval shape about 0.5-cm / ¼-inch thick. Lay them on a greased baking tray and put it on the middle shelf of the oven for 10–15 minutes. Serve with Mumbai Hot Lamb Curry (see page 48) and Tarka Dal (see page 99).

**Tip**
• Add a pinch of ground cinnamon to the dough for extra flavour.

# Chapatis Phulka फुल्का

These are quite tricky to make and many people simply can't be bothered with all the hassle – including me! But nothing compares with a freshly cooked chapati. Similar to the Mexican tortilla, it's a round pan-roasted flat bread made from wholewheat flour. Chapatis are a staple of most Indian households, especially in Britain, and are cooked just before a meal is to be served.

| Serves 2 – about 8 chapatis | Preparation: 5 minutes<br>Cooking: 15 minutes (about 2 minutes per chapati) |
| --- | --- |

450 g / 1 lb wholemeal plain flour

Set aside 200 g / 7 oz flour for shaping the chapatis. Place the rest in a deep bowl and keep 250 ml / 9 fl oz water in a bowl near the flour. Add the water, a little at a time, kneading as you go, until you have a soft, elastic dough. (See page 115 for how to knead dough.) The longer you knead the dough the softer the chapatis will be.

Sprinkle a little flour on to a flat surface or board. Divide the dough into 8, and shape each piece into a ball. Flatten the balls slightly, then place one on the floured board and roll it out into a flat disc approximately 15 cm / 6 in in diameter, flouring the board when necessary. Repeat with the other 7 balls.

Heat a griddle or a shallow frying pan. Lay a disc on the griddle or pan and leave it until the surface is bubbly, 20–30 seconds. Using some tongs, turn it over and cook the other side for 10–15 seconds. As soon as brown spots appear on the underside, the chapati is done. Place a sheet of kitchen paper between each one to absorb the moisture. Take them off the griddle and spread butter over one side, if you like. Serve immediately with Jubilee Curry (see page 29) or Dry Cauliflower and Potato (see page 68) with Butter Lentils (see page 95).

Chapatis can be reheated but they're best cooked fresh. You could also spread your favourite pickle or chutney over them and roll them into tortilla shapes.

# Deep-fried Breads Pooris पूरी

Poori is a fried bread that can be found in Indian fast-food restaurants. It is so versatile that it can be served with practically anything, sweet or savoury, such as *Crème Fraîche* with Saffron (see page 160) or Potatoes with Dried Red Chillies (see page 64).

| Serves 2–3<br>Makes approximately 10 pooris | Preparation: 5 minutes<br>Cooking: 15 minutes |
| --- | --- |
| 500 ml / 18 fl oz oil for frying, or<br> enough to fill your deep-fat fryer | 150 g / 5 oz plain flour<br>20 g / 1 oz butter |

Heat the oil in a deep saucepan or deep-fat fryer. Meanwhile, put the flour, butter and 65 ml / 3 fl oz water in a bowl and mix well, then knead into a dough (see page 115 for how to knead). Add a little extra flour if the dough needs to be firmer. Divide it into 8–10 golf balls. Roll out each ball, on a floured surface, into a small flat disc about 3 mm / ¼ in thick. To check that the oil is hot enough, chop a trimming from the dough into the oil: if it puffs up the oil is ready. Cook the pooris two at a time. Turn them over when they puff up and then, when they turn light brown, which takes about 1 minute, remove them from the oil and place them on a plate with kitchen paper. Repeat the process until you've cooked all of the balls.

You can make pooris in advance and warm them in the oven for a couple of minutes before serving.

### Tips
- Add ¼ teaspoon of cumin or onion seeds while you are preparing the dough.
- Form the dough into 1 large ball, roll it out and cut disc shapes with a pastry cutter of about 7 cm / 3 in in diameter.
- Before frying a poori, fill the centre with 1 tablespoon of a savoury filling such as Minced Lamb with Peas (see page 49). Fold over and seal the poori by pressing around the circumference of the semicircle. Then deep-fry.

# Onion Pancakes
Pyaz Ka Maalpua प्याज़ का मालपुआ

My mum calls these vegetarian pancakes or Indian omelettes because there are no eggs in the batter. My grandmother put them in her school lunch box with some chutney. Her friends couldn't get enough of them!

| Serves 2–4<br>Makes 8–10 pancakes | Preparation: 6 minutes<br>Cooking: 2 minutes per pancake |
|---|---|

| | |
|---|---|
| 1 onion, peeled and chopped | 150 g / 6 oz gram (chickpea) flour |
| 1 chilli, seeded and chopped | 1 tsp cumin seeds |
| 1 tomato, peeled and chopped | ¼ tsp salt |
| 1 tsp peeled and grated root ginger | Vegetable oil for shallow frying |

Put the onion, chilli, tomato and ginger into the blender with 250 ml / 9 fl oz water and whiz until you have a coarse runny paste. Put the flour, cumin seeds and salt into a bowl and mix thoroughly. Then stir in the onion paste. Heat a frying pan, preferably non-stick, and put into it a teaspoon of oil. When it is hot pour in 4 tablespoons of the batter and spread it evenly to make a round shape approximately 15 cm / 6 in in diameter.

After about 30 seconds, flip over the pancake and cook on the other side for the same amount of time. Serve hot with a Coconut and Mustard Chutney (see page 122), Chilli Jelly (see page 133) or Deep-fried Potatoes in Curry Sauce (see page 65).

### Tip
- If you have no gram flour use plain flour, but add a pinch of baking powder to the mixture.

# Chutneys and Dressings
# ९ चटणी

If you check out your local supermarket shelves, you'll discover a vast selection of pickles and chutneys. Most are very good and I cannot resist the mouthwatering temptations with which I am confronted. However, pickling and preserving are ancient Indian customs: during the summer months women prepare their pickles with fruits, vegetables and spices, and swap samples with family, friends and neighbours. I remember my schooldays in India: my best friend's grandmother had a stock of pickles stored in huge jars which we dipped into at tea-time.

Chutneys are made from fresh fruit, vegetables and herbs, which are either chopped, blended or ground together with a little water, vinegar or lemon juice. Chutneys tantalize the tastebuds and traditionally accompany the main meal to add a little zest or provide a sharp contrast. Often they are made on the day that they are eaten. My Fresh Green Coriander Chutney is very quick to make and delicious to eat, and the Mango Chutney more flavoursome than any you can buy.

Salads are easy to prepare and a simple Indian salad dressing consists of a drop of lemon juice, salt, black pepper and a sprinkling of chilli powder. However, I've adapted this with a few ideas to get your creative juices flowing and inspire you to use spices in your dressings.

# Coconut and Mustard Chutney

Nariyal Aur Rai Ki Chatni नारियल और राय की चटणी

This chutney is made predominantly in south India and is served in fast-food restaurants with *dosas* (savoury pancakes) and *idlis* (steamed rice cakes). I used to eat them every day for breakfast! You can use this chutney as a sandwich filler, or serve it with any lentil dish. If you can get hold of some fresh coconuts, the flavour will be sublime.

| Serves 4 | Preparation: 7 minutes   Cooking: 2 minutes |
|---|---|

| | |
|---|---|
| 100 g / 4 oz desiccated coconut *or* fresh grated coconut | 1 tsp groundnut *or* vegetable oil |
| 4 chillies, seeded and roughly chopped | ½ tsp skinned and split black lentils (optional) |
| ½ tsp salt | 1 dried red chilli |
| ¼ tsp cumin seeds | ¼ tsp mustard seeds |
| 1 tsp sugar | 4 curry leaves (optional) |
| 1 tbsp lemon juice | |

If you're using desiccated coconut, soak it in a small bowl with 65 ml / 3 fl oz warm water for a minute. Now put the coconut, desiccated or fresh, into a blender, with 6 tablespoons of water, the fresh chillies, salt, cumin, sugar and lemon juice, and blitz. Empty the contents into a small bowl and set it aside.

Heat the oil in a small pan, and put in the lentils followed by the chilli, mustard seeds and curry leaves. Stir for a minute, then gently pour the mixture over the coconut paste. Serve with Potato and Gram Flour Fritters (see page 17) or with poppadums. The chutney will keep for a week in the fridge.

### Tips
- If you don't have cumin seeds, use ground cumin.
- Curry leaves and black lentils are available from Asian vegetable shops.

# Cucumber Raita

Kachumber Ka Raita कचुम्बर का रायता

Raitas are side dishes served with a main meal and yogurt-based. They're so easy to make and you can include dried fruits, nuts, herbs or vegetables with the yogurt, and various flavourings like a pinch of cumin or black pepper.

| Serves 4 | Preparation: 6 minutes |
|---|---|
| ½ cucumber, washed and grated | 1 green chilli, seeded and finely chopped, or 1 pinch chilli powder |
| 250 ml / 9 fl oz natural yogurt | ½ tsp sugar |
| ¼ tsp salt | 25 g / 1 oz coriander leaves to garnish |

In a bowl mix all of the ingredients together thoroughly, except the coriander leaves. Pour the raita into a serving bowl and scatter over the coriander. Serve chilled with poppadums, or Meatballs in Tomato and Chilli Sauce (see page 54) or Okra with Onions (see page 77).

# Yogurt and Mint Raita

Dahi Pudina Raita दही पुदीना रायता

Here's another basic raita, but you could be adventurous – stir in some finely chopped fresh tomatoes and onions or a teaspoon of mango chutney. Add a seeded chopped chilli for extra zing.

| Serves 4 | Preparation: 2 minutes |
|---|---|
| 250 ml / 9 fl oz natural yogurt | 1 tsp mint sauce or dried mint (or use finely chopped fresh mint) |

Place the yogurt and mint sauce in a bowl and mix thoroughly. Serve chilled with poppadums or with a chicken or vegetable dish.

# Date and Tamarind Chutney Khajoor Aur Imli Ki Chatni खजूर और आमली की चटणी

This chutney is eaten with a Mumbai snack called Bhelpuri – a mixture of puffed rice, green chutneys and nuts. It's an acquired taste of sweet, salty, sour and hot, but it's delicious. It's sold by vendors on beaches.

| Serves 2–4 | Preparation: 8 minutes |
| --- | --- |

100 g / 4 oz dried dates, stoned and chopped

¼ tsp salt

¼ tsp chilli powder

1 tbsp tamarind concentrate

1 tsp vegetable oil

25 g / 1 oz brown sugar

Put all of the ingredients into a blender with 4 tablespoons of water and whiz until you have a fairly smooth paste. Pour it into a bowl and serve with poppadums or Prawn Pakoras (see page 15).

**Tip**
- Instead of brown sugar use the Indian jaggery, a by-product of sugar cane, sold in blocks or large lumps. It tastes richer, musky and caramel-like.

# Fresh Green Coriander Chutney
Dhania Ki Chatni ताजी हरी धनीया की चटणी

This chutney is popular, and can be used as a curry paste too. I often use it in chicken dishes. You can also dip poppadums into it.

| Serves 4 | Preparation: 5 minutes |
|----------|------------------------|

75–100 g / 3–4 oz coriander leaves, washed and coarsely chopped

2 green chillies, seeded and coarsely chopped

1 clove garlic, coarsely chopped

1 tsp root ginger, peeled and grated

Juice of ½ lemon

1 tsp sugar

¼ tsp salt

Put all of the ingredients into the blender and whiz to a thick paste. If it is too dry to process, add a tiny amount of water. Be careful when you open the lid because the strong pungent aroma of the chutney will hit you immediately and may make your eyes water.

Store it in the fridge for 4 days.

## Tips
- Stir the chutney into plain yogurt for a refreshing dip.
- Cover some chicken breasts with the chutney, then sauté or grill them.

# Green Pepper Chutney
Simla Mirch Ki Chatni शिमला मिर्च की चटणी

When my mother spent some time in the Punjab in northern India, she came across various chutneys made from unusual ingredients. Try this one as a relish with cooked ham or cold roasted meat.

| Serves 4 | Preparation: 3 minutes   Cooking: 12 minutes |
|---|---|
| 300 g / 10 oz green peppers, seeded and finely chopped | ¼ tsp turmeric |
| 2 tbsp malt vinegar | ¼ tsp chilli powder |
| 2 tbsp vegetable oil | ¼ tsp garam masala |
| ¼ tsp brown mustard seeds (optional) | ½ tsp salt |
| ¼ tsp cumin seeds | Pinch of ground black pepper |
| | 25 g / 1 oz brown sugar |

Place the peppers in a bowl and stir in the vinegar. Heat the oil in a frying pan and carefully put in the mustard and cumin seeds. When they have popped, add the vinegar-soaked peppers, very carefully, then the turmeric, chilli powder, garam masala, salt and black pepper. Cook the mixture for about 5 minutes or until the peppers are soft. Add the sugar and stir until it has dissolved. Serve hot with pitta bread or poppadums, or on toast. Store in the fridge for 2–3 days.

**Tip**
• If you have no cumin seeds, ground cumin will do.

# Hot Peanut Butter Chutney

Masala Moongfali Chatni मसाला मुन्गफली चटणी

When my mother was a young girl, growing up in India, she loved this peanut chutney with chapatis or on toast.

| Serves 4 | Preparation: 3 minutes |
|---|---|

2 tbsp peanut butter, smooth or crunchy

¼ tsp chilli powder

1 tsp lemon juice

1 clove garlic, peeled and crushed

Mix together all of the ingredients in a bowl, and serve with roast chicken or mashed potato. Store in the fridge for up to a week.

**Tip**

- Use this as a marinade for a quick chicken satay, but add 1 tablespoon of soy sauce.

# Mango Chutney Aam Ki Chatni आम की चटणी

Mango chutney is the most commonly served chutney in Britain's Indian restaurants. The most familiar version has been adapted from a recipe dating back to the early days of the Raj.

| Serves 4 | Preparation: 4 minutes   Cooking: 7 minutes |
|---|---|

| | |
|---|---|
| 2 tbsp vegetable oil | ½ tsp salt |
| 2 dried red chillies | 1 tsp sugar |
| 2 black peppercorns | ¼ tsp paprika |
| Pinch of cumin seeds | 1 tbsp lemon juice |
| ¼ tsp coriander seeds | 1 large ripe mango, peeled, stoned and |
| ¼ tsp onion seeds | coarsely mashed |
| ¼ tsp mustard seeds | |

Heat the oil in a saucepan, and put in the chillies, peppercorns, cumin, coriander, onion and mustard seeds. Let them pop and sizzle, then stir in the salt, sugar and paprika. Carefully add the lemon juice, and cook over a low heat for 1 minute. Now add the mango pulp and cook for 5 minutes. Then allow the chutney to cool and store it in an airtight container in the fridge for up to a week.

**Tip**
• For extra heat, add ¼ teaspoon of chilli powder.

| Chilli and Yogurt Pickle

p.151 | Spicy Nuts

p.143 Carrot Salad

p.162 | Strawberry and Mango Puff

p.161 | Mango Crumble

p.156 | Bread and Butter Pudding with Papaya and Saffron

# Onion Chutney Pyaz Ki Chatni प्याज की चटणी

This is lovely with a lentil dish that doesn't contain too many onions or as a barbecue relish.

| Serves 2–4 | Preparation: 4 minutes   Cooking: 3 minutes |
|---|---|

| | |
|---|---|
| ½ onion, peeled and finely chopped | 1 tsp lemon juice |
| 1 green chilli, seeded and chopped | 1 tsp vegetable oil |
| ¼ tsp salt | ¼ tsp mustard seeds |
| ¼ tsp sugar | |

Put into a blender the onion, chilli, salt, sugar and lemon juice with 2 tablespoons of water and whiz until the contents are smooth.

In a small pan, heat the oil and add the mustard seeds. Once they begin to pop, turn off the heat. Very carefully, add the onion mixture to the pan and stir it well. Serve hot or cold. It goes well with Sugar-Snap Peas with Cumin and Ginger (see page 75).

**Tip**
- Substitute a tomato for the lemon juice.

# Tomato and Chilli Chutney

Tamatar Aur Mirch Ki Chatni टमाटर और मिर्च की चटणी

Delicious with jacket potatoes, papads, or barbecued chicken drumsticks.

| Serves 2–4 | Preparation: 8 minutes |
| --- | --- |

2 tomatoes, finely chopped

6 tbsp tomato ketchup

¼ tsp chilli powder

1 onion, peeled and finely chopped

½ cucumber, finely chopped

½ carrot, peeled and grated

1 beetroot, cooked, peeled and finely chopped (optional)

Pinch of salt (optional)

Mix together all of the ingredients in a bowl and serve. It will keep in the fridge for 4 days.

**Tip**

- If you have no fresh tomatoes use a 200 g / 7 oz can of chopped tomatoes.

# Prawn Balichow
Jhinga Balichow झीन्गा बालीचाव

This is like a prawn pickle and a little goes a long way. Serve it with toast or as an accompaniment to a main dish.

| Serves 2–4 | Preparation: 8 minutes   Cooking: 20 minutes |
|---|---|

| | |
|---|---|
| 4 dried red chillies | ¼ tsp salt |
| 1 large onion, peeled and coarsely chopped | 4–6 cloves garlic, peeled and crushed *or* sliced |
| 4 tbsp malt vinegar | 1 tsp tamarind paste, sieved |
| 1 tsp peeled and grated root ginger | 4 tbsp vegetable *or* groundnut oil |
| ¼ tsp turmeric | 200 g / 7 oz frozen peeled prawns (thawed) |
| ¼ tsp ground cumin | |

Soak the chillies in some warm water for a couple of minutes. Then, apart from the prawns and oil, whiz all the ingredients together in a blender until they are well combined.

Heat 2 tablespoons of the oil in a saucepan, then fry the prawns for a couple of minutes. Take them out of the pan and place them on a dish. Add the remaining 2 tablespoons of oil to what remains in the pan and fry the minced onion mixture for about 6 minutes. The water will evaporate and the mixture should thicken. Then put in the prawns and fry for a couple more minutes. Serve hot or cold, perhaps smeared on some French toast or as a chutney with poppadums. Store in the fridge for 3–4 days.

### Tip
- If you have no dried red chillies, use 1 teaspoon of chilli powder.

# Chilli and Yogurt Pickle
Dahi Mirch Ka Achaar दही मिर्च का अचार

This is very hot so treat it cautiously! I've used the large bullet chillies because they're a milder variety.

| Serves 2–4 | Preparation: 4 minutes   Cooking: 10 minutes |
| --- | --- |

1 tbsp vegetable oil
¼ tsp mustard seeds
¼ tsp turmeric
½ tsp salt
¼ tsp ground coriander
¼ tsp ground cumin

100 g / 4 oz bullet, or Anaheim, green
   chillies, seeded and stalks removed
1 tbsp lemon juice
1 tsp sugar
2 tbsp natural yogurt

In a saucepan, heat the oil and add the mustard seeds. When they begin to sizzle and pop, add the turmeric, salt, coriander and cumin, stir for a minute, then tip in the chillies and stir for another minute. Add the lemon juice and sugar, then stir for 3 minutes. Cover and cook over a low heat for 3 more minutes. Finally, add the yogurt. Serve with chapatis or hot pitta bread as an accompaniment to a mild curry, like Vegetable Korma (see page 62) or Butter Lentils (see page 95).

### Tips
- Use this pickle sparingly with burgers and fries, or bangers and mash.
- You can use 1 tablespoon of Greek-style yogurt mixed with 1 teaspoon of water instead of ordinary natural yogurt.
- For a hotter pickle use thinner chillies, which are more fiery.

# Chilli Jelly Mirch Ki Jelly मिर्च की जेली

I enjoy this jelly with pizza or chips. It's an unusual combination of sweet and spicy. I even spread it on toast. The inspiration behind it is south-west American and Mexican cooking.

| Serves 4<br>Makes about 120 g of Jelly | Preparation: 6 minutes    Cooking: 9 minutes |
| --- | --- |

5 green chillies, seeded and finely
  chopped
5 red chillies, seeded and finely
  chopped

100 g / 4 oz caster sugar
3 tbsp lemon juice
50 ml / 2 fl oz Certo/liquid pectin

Take a heavy-based saucepan and put in the chillies, sugar and lemon juice. Heat slowly until the sugar has dissolved, stirring from time to time. Add the Pectin then bring it rapidly to the boil and let it boil for 2 minutes. Remove the pan from the heat. Allow it to cool a little and stir the jelly to prevent the chillies floating to the top. Pour it into a sterilized jar and cover. The jelly will keep in the fridge for 2–3 months.

**Tip**
- Present the jelly as a special gift to someone who likes it hot!

# Cumin Ketchup Jeera Sauce जीरा सोस

This makes a change from plain tomato ketchup and gives it that home-made touch. My mother occasionally impresses her friends with it: they often think the recipe must be laborious . . .

---

**Preparation: 3 minutes**

| | |
|---|---|
| ½ tsp ground cumin | 4 tbsp tomato ketchup |
| 1 tbsp olive oil | ¼ tsp chilli powder |
| ¼ tsp black pepper | Juice of ½ lemon |

Stir together all the ingredients in a bowl, and serve with fries, Prawn Pakoras (see page 15) or Onion Bhajis (see page 145).

**Tip**
- Add ½ teaspoon of curry powder if you have no cumin.

# Spicy Salad Dressing
Masala Salaad Dressing मसाला सलाद ड्रेसिन्ग

This will brighten up the blandest tomatoes and lettuce leaves.

---

**Preparation: 5 minutes**

| | |
|---|---|
| 1 green chilli, seeded and finely chopped | ½ tsp brown sugar *or* 1 tsp runny honey |
| 4 tbsp balsamic vinegar | 1 tbsp olive oil |
| 1 tsp mustard powder *or* made English mustard | Freshly ground black pepper |
| | 1 tsp lemon juice |
| | ½ tsp cider vinegar |

Put all the ingredients into a jar and screw on the lid. When you're ready to eat, shake it then pour the dressing over the salad and toss.

# Dried Red Chilli Dressing
Laal Mirch Ki Dressing लाल मिर्च की ड्रेसिन्ग

Whole dried chillies have a variety of uses in Indian cuisine, and the potency, or firepower, of a dish depends on how they are treated before cooking. For maximum heat, the stems and seeds are left in.

**Preparation: 5 minutes**

| | |
|---|---|
| 2 dried red chillies, halved lengthwise | 1 tsp runny honey |
| Pinch of salt | 1 tsp olive oil |
| 4 black peppercorns, crushed | Juice of ½ lemon |
| 4 tbsp malt vinegar | |

Pour all of the ingredients into a jar, screw on the lid and shake. Leave the chillies to infuse in the jar for a few minutes, then remove them. When you're ready to eat, shake it again, pour the dressing over the salad and toss.

**Tip**
• Use 1 fresh, seeded and finely chopped red chilli instead of the dry ones.

# Chilli Dressing
## Mirch Ki Dressing मिर्च की ड्रेसिन्ग

Indians will make anything out of chillies, and my friend Lopa will not eat anything unless it's smothered in them. The hotter the better for her. As she can tolerate high levels of heat, this dressing might be a little mild for her.

| Serves 4 | Preparation: 5 minutes |
| --- | --- |

6 black peppercorns, crushed

1 red chilli, seeded and finely chopped

1 tbsp sesame oil

1 tbsp vinegar

1 tbsp lemon juice

1 tsp peeled and grated root ginger

¼ tsp salt

Put all of the ingredients into a jar and screw on the lid. When you're ready to eat, shake it for a few seconds, then pour the dressing over the salad and toss.

**Tip**
- You can use green chillies instead of red. Bullet, or Anaheim, chillies are milder.

# Barbecue and Party Time
# १० बार्बक्यो और पार्टी

Eating alfresco is not the norm in Indian homes, because of the heat and the mosquitoes, although many people buy snacks from street vendors. Come rain or shine, it's a different story in Britain: the barbecue is a ritual of the British summer. It's easy to add a little more fire to your barbecue with some chilli and spice. You can make a hot marinade in minutes to transform the dullest drumsticks and the blandest burgers. Most of the recipes in this chapter can be cooked indoors too and I occasionally eat them when I'm in a hurry as they are so quick and easy to prepare.

When I'm invited to a party held by some Asian mates I know there'll be lots of spicy grub. And, with the exception of music and drink, I think good food is the essential element in a good knees-up. Traditional Indian views on hospitality ensure that we never let our guests leave with empty bellies, and a lot of effort goes into the menu to make sure that everyone is catered for. Why don't you hand round the Paneer Love Bites and Spicy Nuts with drinks for a change, and provide Onion Bhajis or Samosas for later in the evening? Next a fragrant pulao rice and a rich chicken curry will go down well, and don't forget to round things off with something sweet, like an Indian custard or a trifle!

# Lamb Kebabs Seekh Kebab सीग कबाब

Kebabs are often made with small pieces of spiced meat and either grilled or fried. However, these are made with minced lamb and are very popular – the Indian equivalent of burgers. Serve them with a spicy relish.

| Serves 2–3<br>Makes 8–10 kebabs | Preparation: 10 minutes    Cooking: 15 minutes |
|---|---|

| | |
|---|---|
| Juice of ½ lemon | ½ tsp ground coriander |
| 450 g / 1 lb minced lamb | 1 tsp ground cumin |
| 1 tbsp vegetable or olive oil | ½ tsp black peppercorns, crushed |
| 4 cloves garlic, peeled and crushed | ½ tsp turmeric |
| 2 tsp peeled and grated root ginger | ½ tsp garam masala |
| 4 green chillies, seeded and chopped | 1 tsp salt |
| 25 g / 1 oz fresh coriander leaves,<br>   washed and chopped | Oil for grilling |

Have ready 10 skewers. Stir 2 teaspoons of the lemon juice into the mince and set it aside. Then blend together the oil, garlic, ginger, chillies, coriander leaves, the spices, salt and the remaining lemon juice. Fold this paste into the meat.

With wet hands mould the meat into long sausage shapes, then wind each sausage around the skewers, pressing gently. Brush with a little oil and grill under a medium heat or on the barbecue until the meat is cooked right through. Serve with hot pitta bread and Tomato and Chilli Chutney (see page 130).

### Tips
- Add 2 extra chillies for more heat.
- Make flat burgers and call them Shammi Kebabs.
- To cook them in the oven, preheat it to 180°C / 350°F / Gas Mark 4; lay the kebabs on a greased baking tray, baste them with a little oil and cover them in foil. Bake for 20–25 minutes.

# Tikka Kebabs तीका कबाब

Tikka Kebabs are made from lean boneless pieces of meat steeped in a spicy yogurt-based marinade then grilled. My mate Aditya from Haryana makes these all the time.

| Serves 4 | Preparation: 3 minutes, plus 30–120 minutes for marinating<br>Cooking: 15 minutes |
|---|---|

2 tbsp vegetable oil

1 tbsp peeled and grated root ginger

1 tsp lemon juice

¼ tsp ground cumin

Pinch of chilli powder

¼ tsp paprika

¼ tsp ground coriander

¼ tsp turmeric

¼ tsp salt

1 clove garlic, peeled and crushed

2 tbsp natural yogurt

2 chicken breasts, skinned and cut into bite-size pieces

Put all of the ingredients, except the chicken, into a bowl and stir them together. Put in the chicken, stir well, cover and leave in the refrigerator for at least 30 minutes, longer if you have time.

When you're ready to eat them, skewer the chicken pieces and either grill or barbecue them for 12–15 minutes, turning them once. Serve with hot pitta bread and a crisp green salad.

### Tips
- If you have no chilli powder, use a little more paprika.
- Add 25 g / 1 oz finely chopped coriander leaves to the marinade.

# Chicken in a Hot, Sweet 'n' Spicy Marinade

Murg Tikka Mittha Mix मुर्ग तीका मीठा मिक्स

I've thrown in quite a few spices to make up this marinade, including extra cumin and coriander powder. The sweet element is the sugary ketchup, which also gives it that delicious stickiness.

| Serves 4 | Preparation: 3 minutes, plus 2 hours' marinating time<br>Cooking: 15 minutes |
|---|---|

2 tsp paprika

½ tsp ground cumin

½ tsp chilli powder

½ tsp garam masala

½ tsp ground coriander

1 tsp peeled and grated root ginger

4 tbsp tomato ketchup

8 large wings *or* 4 skinless chicken
    breasts, pricked

Mix together all the spices, ginger and ketchup in a large bowl. Add the chicken pieces and coat them thoroughly with the marinade. Cover the bowl and refrigerate for 2 hours or longer if possible. Then barbecue or grill the chicken for 15 minutes until it's thoroughly cooked – the juices will run clear when you stab it with a knife or fork.

**Tip**
- If you don't have all the spices, add 3–4 teaspoons of curry powder instead of the paprika, cumin, coriander and garam masala.

# Chicken Satay Bites
Murg Satay Bite मुर्ग साते बाअीट

I once went for a two-hour cooking lesson in a remote village in Bali. It was great fun, and as I was the only student I had one-to-one teaching and managed to follow all the recipes. This was my favourite.

| Serves 2 | Preparation: 8 minutes |
|----------|------------------------|
|          | Cooking: 15 minutes, plus 2 hours' marinating time or overnight |

1 tsp vegetable oil

2 cloves garlic, peeled and crushed

2 chicken breasts, skinned and cut into
   bite-size pieces

8–10 macadamia nuts, crushed

¼ tsp white pepper

1 green chilli, seeded and finely
   chopped

1 tbsp lemon juice

2 tbsp sweet soy sauce

Pinch of salt

Have ready 8–10 skewers.

Heat the oil in a frying pan, and sauté the garlic. Take a bowl and put into it the chicken, nuts, fried garlic, pepper, chilli, lemon juice, soy sauce and salt. Cover and place in the refrigerator for a couple of hours or overnight.

When you are ready to eat, skewer the meat and grill or barbecue it for 10 minutes.

### Tips
- If you have no macadamia nuts, use 7–8 shelled and skinned peanuts.
- No soy sauce? Use 2 tablespoons of Worcester sauce and 1 teaspoon of honey.

# Corn-on-the-Cob with Couscous Salad

Masala Makki Aur Couscous Ka Salad

मसाला मक्की और कूसकूस का सलाद

Crisp, spicy corn kernels with an aromatic couscous salad. Try it with a dollop of Chilli Jelly (see page 133).

| Serves 4 | Preparation: 5 minutes   Cooking: 10 minutes |
|---|---|

| | |
|---|---|
| 4 corn cobs | *For the Couscous Salad* |
| *For the dressing* | 50 g / 2 oz couscous |
| 2 cloves garlic, peeled and crushed | 1 tbsp olive oil |
| Juice of 1 lemon | ¼ tsp onion seeds |
| ¼ tsp salt | 4 curry leaves |
| 1 tsp sugar | ¼ tsp salt |
| 1 green chilli, seeded and finely | 8 roasted peanuts, skinned and |
|   chopped |   crushed |
| ¼ tsp ground black pepper | 25 g / 1 oz fresh coriander leaves, |
| 1 tbsp runny honey |   washed and chopped, to garnish |

First, make the dressing. Put all of the ingredients into a jar with a lid. Shake well, and brush it on to the corn cobs just before you barbecue or grill them. They will be ready when the kernels are tender and lightly browned.

For the couscous salad, bring to the boil 500 ml / 18 fl oz water with a dash of oil. Stir in the couscous, cover and let it stand for 5 minutes. Meanwhile, heat the oil in a small pan, then put in the onion seeds, curry leaves, salt and peanuts. Stir for a minute then add the couscous and cook gently for 4 minutes. Scrape the couscous into a serving bowl, scatter over the coriander and serve with the corn.

### Tips
- No green chillies? Add another ¼ teaspoon of ground black pepper.
- No onion seeds? Substitute 4 finely chopped spring onions.

# Carrot Salad

Gaajar Ka Koshimbir गाजर का कोशिम्बिर

This dish is from Mumbai in Maharashtra. As a teenager my mum ate it almost every day with her family. It's hot but refreshing.

| Serves 2 | Preparation: 10 minutes |
|---|---|

2 carrots, peeled and grated

½ onion, peeled and finely chopped

1 tomato, finely chopped

1 green chilli, seeded and finely chopped

1 tbsp roasted peanuts, crushed

½ tsp sugar

1 tbsp lemon juice

¼ tsp salt

1 tsp olive *or* groundnut oil

¼ tsp black mustard seeds

2 fresh curry leaves

¼ tsp turmeric

Stir together in a bowl the carrots, onion, tomato, chilli, peanuts, sugar, lemon juice and salt, and set it aside.

Heat the oil in a pan, then add the mustard seeds and curry leaves. Let them sizzle and pop, then stir in the turmeric. Carefully pour the spicy mixture into the carrot salad. Stir well and serve immediately, with Garlic and Ginger Chicken (see page 37) or Tarka Dal (see page 99) and pitta bread.

### Tips

- If you have no fresh tomatoes, substitute a 200 g / 7 oz can of chopped ones.
- No green chillies? Add a pinch of chilli powder.
- Use cabbage instead of carrots for a change.

# Jacket Potato Filling

Bhara Aloo Masala भरा आलू मसाला

This is my idea of a fast-food snack – there's little cooking or preparation involved. It tastes better than burgers and it's homemade.

| Serves 2 | Preparation: 4 minutes   Cooking: 8 minutes |
|----------|---------------------------------------------|

1 tbsp olive oil

½ onion, peeled and chopped

Pinch of chilli powder

¼ tsp turmeric

¼ tsp curry powder *or* curry paste

200 g / 7 oz can Spam, cubed

200 g / 7 oz can baked beans

Heat the oil in a saucepan, then put in the onion and fry until brown. Add the chilli powder, turmeric and curry powder or paste and stir them into the onions. Then put in the Spam and sauté for a minute. Stir in the beans and cook for another minute. Serve hot on a jacket potato with a crisp green salad, or with fries or pitta bread.

**Tip**
- Chop up a cooked vegetarian sausage and stir into the beans instead of Spam.

# Onion Bhajis Pyaz Kay Pakoray प्याज के पकोड़े

Rich golden clusters of onion and hot spices bound in a crisp batter. Savour them at any time. Straight from the pan, they're very moreish . . .

| Serves 2–4 | Preparation: 6 minutes | Cooking: 4 minutes |
| --- | --- | --- |

| | |
| --- | --- |
| Vegetable oil, for deep frying | ¼ tsp coriander seeds, crushed |
| 1 onion, peeled and sliced | ¼ tsp cumin seeds |
| 1 green chilli, seeded and finely chopped | 50 g / 2 oz gram (chickpea) flour |
| | ¼–½ tsp salt |

Heat the oil in a deep saucepan or a deep-fat fryer.

In a bowl mix together the rest of the ingredients with 2 tablespoons of water to make a stiff, thick batter. If it seems too runny, add some more flour.

The temperature of the oil is important. To check whether it is hot enough, add a tablespoon from the pan to the bhaji mixture. If it sizzles, the oil is ready. Slowly place teaspoon-size drops of the mixture into the oil, 5–6 at a time, depending on the size of the pan. They take about a minute to cook and should turn golden. When they have cooled they will be crunchy. Take them out of the oil and place them on a plate covered with kitchen paper. Taste one before you fry the whole batch, and adjust the seasoning if necessary. Serve hot with tomato ketchup or Yogurt and Mint Raita (see page 123).

**Tip**
- For puffball bhajis, add a pinch of bicarbonate of soda to the batter.

# Garlic, Chilli and Mushroom Bhaji

Lasooni Aur Mirch Ki Guchchiya

लसुनी और मिर्च की गुच्छिया

A variation on garlic mushrooms!

| Serves 4–6 | Preparation: 3 minutes   Cooking: 10 minutes |
|---|---|

500 g / 1 lb 2 oz closed-cup
   mushrooms
Pinch of black pepper

4 cloves garlic, peeled and crushed
25 g / 1 oz butter
4 green chillies, seeded and finely
   chopped

Preheat the oven to 180°C / 350°F / Gas Mark 4. Place the mushrooms on a baking tray and sprinkle them with some pepper, the chillies and the garlic. Then melt the butter, drizzle it over them and bake for 10 minutes. Serve with Chilli Jelly (see page 133).

**Tip**
- Alternatively, put all of the ingredients into a frying pan and sauté for 5 minutes.

# Samosas समोसा

Samosas are popular all over India and in Britain. Indian samosas are usually filled with potato but sometimes you'll find them with carrots, peas, sultanas and even chocolate. They take time to prepare but once you get the hang of it, there'll be no stopping you. It's advisable and safer to use a deep-fat fryer with a thermostat control to cook them.

| Makes 8–10 samosas | Preparation: 15 minutes   Cooking: 40 minutes |
|---|---|

*For the filling*
2 tbsp vegetable oil
1 onion, peeled and chopped
2 green chillies, seeded and finely chopped
¼ tsp salt
Pinch of garam masala
¼ tsp ground cumin
¼ tsp ground coriander

300 g / 10 oz potatoes, peeled, boiled and roughly mashed
25 g / 1 oz fresh coriander leaves, washed and chopped
*For the pastry*
700 g / 7 oz plain flour, plus a little extra
1 tsp oil
Pinch of salt

First, make the filling. Heat the oil in a saucepan then fry the onion and chillies for 5 minutes until they're soft. Add the salt, garam masala, cumin and coriander, and stir-fry for a minute. Then tip in the mashed potato and stir well to blend the ingredients together. Turn off the heat, then fold in the chopped coriander leaves and set aside.

Now make the pastry. Put the flour, oil, salt and 6–7 tablespoons of water into a bowl, and mix it into a dough.

In a small bowl or cup, mix together a little flour and water to make a glue, like paste. Divide the dough into pieces and, on a floured surface, roll them out into thin rounds about 3 mm/⅛ in thick. Cut each round in half. Carefully lift one of the semicircles and apply the 'glue' to the straight edge, then fold it to make a cone shape, sealing the pasted straight edge. Lift the cone, with the tapered end at the bottom, and fill it with the potato mixture. Seal the samosa with a little more glue. Repeat, until all of the pastry has been used up.

Heat the oil in a deep-fat fryer to around 180°C/350°F. To check that the oil is hot enough, drop in a tiny piece of dough: if it sizzles and surfaces, the oil is ready. Carefully place the samosas, a few at a time, in the hot oil and fry for 3–4 minutes until golden brown. Take them out and leave them to drain on kitchen paper in a warm place (perhaps the oven turned to the lowest setting) while you cook the rest.

Serve hot with Fresh Green Coriander Chutney (see page 125) or tomato ketchup.

### Tips
- Use up any leftover vegetables in the filling.
- Stuff the samosas with cooked spiced beef or Minced Lamb with Peas (see page 49) for a change.

# Paneer Love Bites Paneer Pasanda पनीर पसन्दा

This is a fun finger-food recipe. In love potions coriander was said to fill those who drank them with desire.

| Serves 2–4 | Preparation: 5 minutes   Cooking: 5 minutes |
|---|---|

2 tbsp vegetable oil

1 tsp coriander seeds, crushed

1 tsp cumin seeds, crushed

250 g / 8 oz paneer cheese, cubed

3 cloves garlic, peeled and crushed

2 green chillies, stalks removed, seeded
　and cut lengthways

¼ tsp salt

½ tsp chilli powder

2 tbsp soy sauce

4 spring onions, sliced, for garnish

Heat the oil in a wok or large frying pan, then put in the coriander and cumin seeds. Allow them to sizzle and pop for a few moments. Stir in the cheese and fry for a couple of minutes until its edges begin to brown. Add the garlic, green chillies and salt and stir for another 2 minutes. Finally sprinkle in the chilli powder and soy sauce, and stir, then take the pan off the heat. Spear each paneer cube on a cocktail stick, and set them on a plate. Scatter over the spring onions and serve with Onion Chutney (see page 129) or Tomato and Chilli Chutney (see page 130).

# Nachos with Cumin and Chilli

Masala Nachos मसाला नाचोस

My mother is quite particular when it comes to food, but she was delighted with this snack. The tortillas are smothered with melting cheese, tangy tomatoes, hot chillies and crunchy onion. A substantial treat to quell hunger pangs.

| Serves 2–4 | Preparation: 4 minutes   Cooking: 6–7 minutes |
|---|---|
| 100 g / 4 oz spicy tortilla chips | ½ onion, peeled and finely chopped |
| 50–75 g / 2–3 oz Cheddar cheese, grated | 1 small tomato, finely chopped |
| ¼ tsp ground cumin | 2 green chillies, seeded and finely chopped |

Cover a baking tray with tortilla chips and spread the cheese evenly on top. Sprinkle over the cumin, onion, tomato and chillies. Place under the grill for 6–7 minutes. Serve with Tomato and Chilli Chutney (see page 130) or Chilli and Avocado Dip (see page 154).

### Tip
- Top with cooked, shredded chicken or Minced Lamb with Peas (see page 49) to make a substantial first course.

# Spicy Nuts Masala Moongfali मसाला मुन्गफली

These are perfect with alcohol!

| Serves 4–6 | Preparation: 3 minutes | Cooking: 7 minutes |
|---|---|---|

| | |
|---|---|
| 2 tbsp vegetable oil | ¼ tsp garam masala |
| 100 g / 4 oz natural shelled peanuts | ½ tsp chilli powder |
| 100 g / 4 oz natural shelled almonds | ¼ tsp salt |
| 100 g / 4 oz natural roasted cashew nuts | |

Heat the oil in a saucepan, then fry the peanuts for about 2 minutes. Take them out with a slotted spoon, and put them on kitchen paper to absorb the oil. Repeat with the almonds, in the same pan, and then the cashew nuts, but fry the latter for 1 minute. Put all of the nuts into a bowl, then stir in the garam masala, chilli powder and salt. Let them cool and serve with chilled beer.

**Tip**
- Add another ¼ teaspoon of chilli powder for more zing. Put in some shelled pistachios, if you like, for variety.

# Peanuts in Gram Flour

Besan Ki Moongfali बेसन की मुन्गफली

Another moreish mouthful. Once you start on these you'll find it hard to stop.

| Serves 2 | Preparation: 3 minutes  Cooking: 4 minutes |
|---|---|
| Vegetable oil, for deep frying | Pinch of turmeric |
| ¼ tsp chilli powder | ¼ tsp salt |
| ¼ tsp cumin seeds | 25 g / 1 oz gram (chickpea) flour |
| Pinch of coriander seeds | 2 tbsp dry-roasted peanuts |

Heat the oil gently in a large saucepan.

Put into a bowl the chilli powder, cumin and coriander seeds, turmeric, salt and gram flour. Add 1 tablespoon of water, and stir it all into a thick paste. Add the peanuts.

Now check that the oil is hot enough: with a spatula, carefully drop a little into the batter. If it splatters or pops, it is ready. Drop the coated peanuts into the oil and fry for a few seconds or until they are knobbly and golden brown. Serve as a snack with Tomato and Chilli Chutney (see page 130).

### Tips

- If you have no chilli powder use ½ teaspoon of paprika or a fresh green chilli, seeded and chopped.
- Reheat for 5–7 minutes at 160°C / 325°F / Gas Mark 3 if you want to serve them hot.

# Vol-au-vent Filling वोल ओ वोन्ट फिलिन्ग

Although vol-au-vents are European, they make the perfect vehicle for a spicy filling. Surprise your friends!

| Serves 4<br>Enough to fill 16 vol-au-vent cases | Preparation: 3 minutes<br>Cooking: 10 minutes |
|---|---|

16 frozen vol-au-vent cases

1 tbsp olive oil

100 g / 4 oz mushrooms, finely
   chopped

3–4 cloves garlic, peeled and crushed

Pinch of salt

¼ tsp chilli powder

½ tsp sugar

3 tsp sour cream

Prepare the vol-au-vent cases as instructed on the packet and bake them while you make the filling.

Heat the oil in a saucepan, then fry the mushrooms and garlic for 2 minutes. Add the salt, chilli powder and sugar, and stir well for a minute. Take the pan off the heat and leave it to cool for a few minutes. Then fold in the sour cream. Use the mixture to fill the vol-au-vents and serve either hot or cold.

**Tip**
- For a dash of colour and extra flavour, scatter some finely chopped coriander leaves over each vol-au-vent.

# Chilli and Garlic Butter

Mirch Aur Lasooni Butter मिर्च और लसुनी बटर

A piquant variation on a faithful standard!

| Serves 2–4 | Preparation: 5 minutes |
|---|---|

50 g / 2 oz softened butter

1 green chilli, seeded and finely chopped

1 clove garlic, peeled and crushed

1 baguette

Put the butter into a bowl with the chilli and garlic and beat them together thoroughly. Spoon it into a ramekin or small dish. Spread it on toast, or make garlic-and-chilli bread by spreading it inside a baguette and baking at 140°C / 275°F / Gas Mark 1 for 8–10 minutes.

**Tip**
- Add ¼ teaspoon of coarsely ground black pepper for even more fire.

# Chilli and Avocado Dip

Mirch Aur Avocado Ki Dip मिर्च और एवोकाडो की दिप

This dip gives a real kick to the back of your throat and is great with tortilla chips. It's like an extra-hot guacamole.

| Serves 2–4 | Preparation: 5 minutes |
|---|---|

1 ripe avocado, halved and stoned

2 tbsp sour cream

Pinch of chilli powder

Pinch of salt

2 tsp lemon juice

Scoop the avocado flesh into a bowl and mash it thoroughly with the rest of the ingredients. Serve chilled.

# Desserts
# ११ मीठा

Perhaps you are only familiar with the fudge-like Indian sweets sold in British Asian shops. However, there are many more Indian desserts, delicately flavoured puddings scented with aromatic spices, sweetmeats made of milk cooked until it thickens (*khoya*) and others of nuts and dried fruit, vegetables, even pulses, and dressed with silver and gold leaf. Sweets play an important role in India's customs and traditions. During Diwali, the Festival of Lights, Indian households buy large amounts of rice, sugar, flour, nuts and other vegetarian ingredients to make the traditional sweets, whose preparation is an art form. I love the milk fudge, *barfi*, and the gram-flour-based *besan ki laddoo*. However, even the best cooks buy them ready-made: the cooking processes are so time-consuming. Most Indian desserts, however, take little time to put together.

As Indians have a sweeter tooth than westerners, I've reduced the sugar content in most recipes and created some unusual new ones with a spicy twist. *Srikhand* is a Maharashtrian dessert, but I've made it with *crème fraîche* – it tastes divine. Creamy Apricot Dessert is an indulgence for a special occasion, but when you've tried the Almond Biscuits you'll want to have them around all the time!

# Bread and Butter Pudding with Papaya and Saffron

Papita Aur Kesar Ki Mittha Double Roti

पपीता और केसर की मीठा डबल रोटी

The traditional British Bread and Butter Pudding is without a doubt a firm favourite, but I've added an Indian twist and come up with an impressive dessert for a dinner party. I've substituted papaya for the sultanas or raisins. But you could also try dried apricots or even mangoes.

| Serves 4 | Preparation: 15 minutes Cooking: 30–35 minutes |
|---|---|

| | |
|---|---|
| 250 ml / 9 fl oz double cream | 6 slices white bread, buttered and |
| 65 ml / 3 fl oz milk | sliced into 4 triangles |
| 50 g / 2 oz caster sugar | 50 g / 2 oz ready-to-eat dried papaya, |
| 3–4 saffron strands | finely chopped |
| 3 eggs | 25 g / 1 oz pistachio nuts, crushed |
| A little butter for greasing | |

Preheat the oven to 180°C / 350°F / Gas Mark 4.

Mix the cream with the milk and add the sugar and saffron strands. Whisk the eggs and add them to the cream mixture. Butter a deep ovenproof dish 15 cm × 22 cm / 6 in × 9 in, put into it a layer of bread, then sprinkle over some papaya and nuts. Add another layer of bread then some more nuts and papaya. Pour the cream mixture over the bread and put the dish into the oven for 30–35 minutes, until the surface is a rich golden brown. Serve immediately.

**Tip**
- Add a pinch of nutmeg and another of cinnamon to the cream mixture.

# Creamy Apricot Dessert
Malai Khubani मलाय खुबानी

If you like your desserts not too sweet then this is for you. Cardamoms are used in many Indian preparations both sweet and savoury. In this dish, the subtle flavour of the cardamom complements the apricot.

| Serves 2 | Preparation: 5 minutes   Cooking: 2 minutes |
|---|---|
| 50 g / 2 oz dried apricots, stoned and chopped | Pinch of ground cardamom (optional) |
| 140 ml / 5 fl oz whipped cream | 1 tsp unsalted butter |
| | 5–6 cashew nuts |

Put the apricots into the blender with 2 tablespoons of water and whiz them to a coarse pulp.

In a bowl, whip the cream until it is stiff then add the cardamom (if using). Heat the butter in a saucepan and fry the cashew nuts for 2 minutes. Take them out of the pan and leave them to cool on some kitchen paper, then crush them. Fold the apricot pulp into the cream with the nuts. Serve chilled with Italian biscuits or ice-cream wafers.

**Tip**
- Use dried mango slices instead of apricots, or any other dried fruit.

# Semolina Dessert with Banana
Sheera केले का शीरा

This dish is prepared and offered in Hindu temples after prayers. It's known in Hindi as *prasad*. There are many varieties but this is my favourite – my mother makes it from time to time. I have reduced the sugar content considerably!

| Serves 2–4 | Preparation: 2 minutes   Cooking: 6 minutes |
|---|---|
| 250 g / 8 oz semolina | 1 banana, roughly mashed |
| 50 g / 2 oz unsalted butter | 2 tbsp single or double cream |
| 100 g / 4 oz sugar | 4 green cardamom pods |

Mix the semolina and butter in a saucepan on a medium heat, stirring constantly, for about 5 minutes. You will begin to smell the lovely fragrant aroma. Carefully add 500 ml / 18 fl oz just-boiled water, then the sugar, the banana and cream. Stir over the heat for a minute. Most of the water will be absorbed by the semolina. Crush the cardamoms, discard the husks and stir in the seeds. Serve immediately, with more cream!

# Indian Rice Pudding Kheer खीर

Rice plays an integral role in Indian culture and lifestyle, and at many Hindu festivals it is served to eat and used in colourful rituals. On New Year's day, sweet rice pudding is served to mark a new beginning.

| Serves 4 | Preparation: 4 minutes   Cooking: 16 minutes |
|---|---|
| 5 pistachio nuts, shelled | 100 g / 4 oz basmati rice, rinsed thoroughly |
| 5 almonds, shelled | |
| 600 ml / 1 pint full cream milk | 4 green cardamoms, husks discarded |
| | 1 tbsp sugar |

Soak the nuts in hot water for a couple of minutes then skin and chop them. Place the milk and rice in a saucepan and cook over a medium heat for 12 minutes. Stir occasionally so that the grains don't stick to the bottom of the pan and the milk doesn't boil over.

Then add the nuts and the cardamom seeds and stir for 1 minute, as the milk and rice bubble away gently. Tip in the sugar and stir well for 2 minutes. Turn off the heat, and serve hot or chilled.

**Tip**
- Sprinkle some grated chocolate over the top or add a few sultanas just before serving. If you add sultanas, reduce the sugar by half.

# Indian Custard Desi Custard देसी कस्टड

Even though this is a very simple dish it's considered a treat in India. I've used tinned mango but if you can get a fresh sweet one then all the better.

| Serves 4 | Chilling: 30 minutes   Cooking: 3 minutes |
|---|---|

| | |
|---|---|
| 400 g / 14 oz carton full cream milk custard | 2 green cardamoms, slightly crushed |
| 1 tbsp double cream | 400 g / 14 oz can mango slices, drained and chopped |

Empty the custard into a saucepan, then stir in the cream and the crushed cardamoms. Warm the custard over a very low heat for about 2½ minutes. Do not let it boil. When the custard is hot, remove the cardamoms and pour it into a bowl. Tip in the mangoes, stir, and place the bowl in the refrigerator. Chill for 30 minutes. Serve it with more cream if you dare.

**Tips**
- Use a pinch of powdered cardamom if you haven't any pods.
- Mango slices can be replaced with other fruits, like pineapple, blueberries or grapes.

# *Crème Fraîche* with Saffron
Kesari Srikhand केसरी स्रीखन्ड

This sweet dessert comes from Maharashtra, the state whose capital is Mumbai. *Srikhand* is so popular that it is also commercially available and served in tubs like ice cream.

| Serves 2 | Preparation: 10 minutes |
|---|---|

| | |
|---|---|
| 3–4 saffron strands | 2 tsp caster sugar |
| 4 tbsp milk, warmed | Pinch of nutmeg |
| 150 g / 6 oz *crème fraîche* | 25 g / 1 oz grated chocolate |
| 1 tbsp thick double cream | Bowl of strawberries (optional) |

Put the saffron into a cup with the milk and leave it to soak for a couple of minutes. Whisk together the *crème fraîche*, double cream, sugar and nutmeg until the mixture stiffens. Gently stir in the milk and saffron. The colour of the saffron will turn the dessert a very light yellowy gold. Sprinkle some grated chocolate over the top and chill for 5 minutes. Dip your strawberries – or anything else that takes your fancy! – into it.

### Tip
- Just before serving fold in 2 tablespoons of mango pulp, available in cans, and serve with Italian biscuits instead of strawberries.

# Mango Crumble Aam Crumble आम क्रम्बल

In my junior-school days, we occasionally made apple crumble in cookery lessons. I found this daunting because we never made puddings like that at home. Here is my spicy variation on the traditional recipe.

| Serves 2 | Preparation: 10 minutes   Cooking: 34–44 minutes |
|---|---|

| *For the filling* | Pinch of ground cloves *or* 2 whole |
|---|---|
| 1 large sweet ripe mango, peeled and | cloves |
| sliced (see page xxviii) | *For the crumble* |
| 25 g / 1 oz brown sugar | 150 g / 6 oz plain flour |
| Pinch of nutmeg | 35 g / 1½ oz butter |
| ¼ tsp ground cinnamon | 50 g / 2 oz brown sugar |

Preheat the oven to 180°C / 350°F / Gas Mark 4.

Make the filling: place the mango slices in a saucepan with the sugar, nutmeg, cinnamon and cloves and cook for 5 minutes. Take the pan off the heat.

Now make the crumble: put the flour into a large mixing bowl and rub the butter into the flour with your fingertips until the mixture resembles breadcrumbs. Stir in the sugar.

Spoon the mango mixture into a buttered ovenproof dish and sprinkle over the crumble topping. Bake for 30–40 minutes until the topping is golden brown. Serve with vanilla ice cream or *crème fraîche*.

**Tip**
- If you have no fresh mango, use a tin of mangoes, apricots or peaches, drained.

# Strawberry and Mango Puff
Strawberry Aur Aum Ki Pastry स्ट्रोबरी और आम की पेस्ट्री

Crisp light pastry filled with rich, juicy fruit. This is so simple to make but it tastes heavenly.

| Serves 4 | Preparation: 8 minutes   Baking: 20 minutes |
|----------|---------------------------------------------|

350 g / 12 oz ready-made puff pastry

Knob of butter

1 tbsp caster sugar

200 g / 7 oz can mango slices, chopped

200 g / 7 oz strawberries, hulled, washed and halved

Pinch of grated nutmeg

1 egg, beaten

Preheat the oven to 200°C / 400°F / Gas Mark 6. Grease a baking sheet.

On a floured surface, roll out the pastry and cut it into two rectangles.

Melt the butter in a saucepan and add the sugar, mango, strawberries and nutmeg, then cook for 4 minutes.

Brush the edges of the two pastry rectangles with a little water. Spoon the cooked fruit in the middle of each piece, then fold over the pastry. Seal the 3 sides by pressing down the edges. Brush the tops with some beaten egg. Place them on the baking sheet, put them into the oven and bake for 20 minutes. They will puff up and turn a glossy golden brown. Serve hot with cream.

**Tip**
• You can use any fruit filling, but if you use a can do not add the sugar.

# Mango and Nutmeg Coulis

Aam Aur Jaiphal Ka Sauce आम और जायफल का सोस

A coulis is a thin purée sauce, a French classic to which I have added an exotic touch.

| Serves 4 | Preparation: 2 minutes Cooking: 3 minutes |
|---|---|

| | |
|---|---|
| 1 tbsp unsalted butter *or* ghee (see page xxviii) | 2 black peppercorns |
| | 700 g / 1½ lb can mango pulp |
| 4 whole cloves | Pinch of grated nutmeg |

Heat the butter or ghee in a saucepan, add the cloves and peppercorns and stir for a minute. Pour in the mango pulp, then stir, add the nutmeg and stir again. Take the pan off the heat and leave it to cool. Serve with vanilla ice cream, or pour over a pastry- or sponge-based pudding.

**Tip**
- Soak a few strands of saffron then add them to the mango pulp.

# Chocolate Cake with Cardamom and Pistachio

Elaichi Aur Pista Ka Chocolate Cake

ऑलायची और पिस्ता का चोकलेट केक

I love cake and I love chocolate, I love nuts and I love the flavour of cardamom! So I've put them all into one recipe and baked a really spicy cake!

| Preparation: 5 minutes | Baking: approximately 20 minutes |
|---|---|

- 1 × 250 g / 8 oz packet ready-to-mix chocolate sponge
- 2 green cardamom pods, husks discarded and seeds crushed
- ¼ tsp ground cinnamon (optional)
- 1 tbsp pistachio nuts, shelled and crushed

Prepare the cake mix according to the manufacturer's instructions, but fold in the cardamom and cinnamon, if using. Stir in the pistachio nuts just before you turn the mixture into the tin. Bake as instructed on the packet. Serve hot with a dollop of whipped cream or cold with a mug of tea.

### Tip
- Make a chocolate icing with 65 g / 3 oz butter, 3 tablespoons milk, 25 g / 1 oz cocoa powder, 250 g / 8 oz icing sugar and a generous pinch of grated nutmeg, beaten together. Add the milk gradually – you may not need it all.

# Almond Biscuits Nan Khatai नान खटाई

In India these biscuits are made fresh every day and sold in large bakeries. You can buy the almond syrup in coffee bars around the UK.

| Makes 16 biscuits | Preparation: 10 minutes   Cooking: 15 minutes |
|---|---|

200 g / 7 oz unsalted butter *or* ghee, softened

100 g / 4 oz sugar

350 g / 12 oz plain flour

2 tsp almond syrup

Preheat the oven to 180°C / 350°F / Gas Mark 4.

In a bowl, cream together the butter and sugar, then mix in the flour to make a soft dough. Now stir in the almond syrup. The dough may be a bit crumbly but don't worry: knead it to blend the ingredients together. Grease a flat baking tray or lay a sheet of greaseproof paper over it. Roll the dough to about 0.5 cm / ¼ inch thick and cut out small oval shapes. Place them on the tray so that they don't touch, then bake for 15 minutes, until the biscuits are golden brown. Check the oven from time to time to make sure that they don't burn. Allow them to cool, then store in an airtight container.

### Tips
- Before placing the biscuits in the oven, scatter some chopped almonds over the top.
- Use a few drops of vanilla essence or even ground cardamom instead of almond syrup.
- Make the biscuits star-shaped, or whatever, with a pastry cutter. Put them in a jar as a gift.

# Cumin Biscuits Jeera Biscuit जीरा बिस्कुट

Whenever a guest turns up at the door of an Indian household, even a plumber, they are offered tea or water, usually accompanied by a savoury snack, such as Bombay Mix, spiced peanuts or salty biscuits. These cumin biscuits are normally deep-fried but I've reduced the fat content by baking them.

| Makes 20 biscuits | Preparation: 10 minutes   Cooking: 12 minutes |
| --- | --- |

100 g / 4 oz plain flour
50 g / 2 oz butter, cold
½ tsp cumin seeds

¼ tsp salt
5 tbsp milk

Preheat the oven to 190°C / 375°F / Gas Mark 5.

Sift the flour into a bowl, then rub in the butter with your fingertips. Add the cumin seeds, salt and milk, and knead into a soft, pliable dough.

Roll it out, on a lightly floured surface, to about 0.5 cm / ¼ in thick, then use a 4 cm / 1½ inches cutter to stamp out the biscuits. Grease a baking sheet or line one with greaseproof paper. Place the biscuits on it fairly close together, and bake on a high shelf for 10–12 minutes or until the biscuits are light brown. Allow them to cool completely then store in an airtight container. They keep fresh for about 2 weeks.

**Tip**
- Add a few crushed nuts and ¼ teaspoon of ground black pepper to the dough.

# Drinks
## १२ पेय

Indians enjoy a variety of drinks from aromatic and fragrant to spicy. Like Indian food, many Indian drinks are intended to have either a heating or cooling effect on the body and often to stimulate the mind. The long and hot summers make ice-cold drinks a necessity rather than a luxury – they're recommended as an antidote to sunstroke. Yogurt has a cooling effect, and is a key ingredient in the famed frothy *lassis* of northern India, which are either sweetened or salted. One glass is never enough. Another favourite of the north is Jal Jeera, made with cumin and tamarind. Some Indian drinks are fragrant with aromatic spices, such as cloves, cinnamon and cardamom, or flower essences, like rose. *Sharbats* are made from extracts of herbs, spices and flowers in a sugar syrup, then diluted with milk or water. Milk is combined with almond and saffron to make a sweet and spicy shake for the summer.

There is also a wide variety of fruit drinks ranging from freshly squeezed sugarcane juice to mango and guava. Coffee is sought after, but generally more popular in the south of India, while spiced teas are renowned in the north. I like to throw a few spices into my morning cuppa for a lighter version of the stewed, sweet concoctions served in railway stations across India. More widespread is Indian-style lemonade. Quick to make, it has a cooling effect, like my Virgin Punch.

Few drinks, apart from water, appear with meals. Nevertheless, specific drinks are served on special occasions such as at weddings and religious festivals.

Wines are beginning to appear on restaurant menus with useful suggestions on which best accompanies a particular dish. Indians love the odd tipple and are keen on spirits, such as gin, whisky and rum. There is a home-grown brew of cashew or palm extract, Fenny, which is popular in Goa. I look forward to sampling this on my next visit there!

# Indian Virgin Punch Sharbat शरबत

| Serves 4 | Preparation: 5 minutes |
| --- | --- |

Juice of ½ lemon

250 ml / 9 fl oz orange juice

250 ml / 9 fl oz mango juice

250 ml / 9 fl oz apple juice

330 ml / 12 fl oz sparkling lemonade

250 g / 8 oz mandarin segments,
   drained

Pinch of black pepper (optional)

Stir together all the ingredients in a large jug or bowl and add some ice cubes. Serve immediately with Spicy Nuts (see page 151).

### Tip

- You can use pineapple juice instead of orange and soda water instead of lemonade.

# Indian Lemonade Nimbu Pani निम्बू पानी

In the hot areas of India, this drink is served in restaurants as a thirst-quencher. Nothing else, including commercial fizzy drinks, is quite so refreshing on a hot day.

| Serves 4 | Preparation: 6 minutes |
| --- | --- |

Juice of 2 lemons

Pinch of salt

4 tbsp icing sugar

2 tsp rose water (optional)

Stir together all the ingredients in a large jug and add 500 ml / 18 fl oz water. Drop in a few ice cubes or serve chilled.

### Tip

- Garnish with a few cucumber and lemon slices, and mint leaves.

# Indian Yogurt Smoothie Lassi लस्सी

One of the most popular Indian drinks. It is made either sweet or salted and occasionally prepared with spices. I prefer mine simple and sweet. Once you've started drinking it, you just can't stop!

| Serves 2 | Preparation: 5 minutes |
|----------|------------------------|

125 ml / 4 fl oz milk          2 tsp sugar
175 ml / 6 fl oz natural yogurt

Put all the ingredients into a blender and whiz. Pour into glasses and add some ice cubes.

### Tips
- Add a couple of drops of vanilla essence or some of your favourite soft fruit, for example, banana or strawberries.
- For a creamier, thicker drink, add 2 tablespoons of cream before whizzing in the blender.
- For a salty lassi, add ½ teaspoon of grated ginger and a pinch of salt, then sprinkle with ground black pepper before serving.

# Almond and Saffron Milk
## Basundi बासुन्ढी

*Basundi* is served at weddings and parties. It's very rich, very creamy and luxurious. It tastes quite nutty and is lovely as a morning pick-me-up or a nightcap.

| Serves 2 | Preparation: 2 minutes   Cooking: 5 minutes |
| --- | --- |

500 ml / 18 fl oz full cream milk

2 tsp sugar

4–5 saffron strands

1 tsp ground almonds

4 pistachio nuts, shelled and lightly crushed

2 almonds, shelled and lightly crushed

Heat the milk, sugar and saffron in a saucepan for 4 minutes, but do not let it boil, stirring occasionally. Add the ground almonds and cook for 1 minute. Then turn off the heat and add the pistachios and almonds. Serve warm or cold.

**Tip**
- Crush the almonds and pistachio nuts by placing them under a saucepan and pressing down on them, or use a rolling pin.

# Buttermilk Chaas छास

A refreshing drink served with lunch in summer. Slimmers drink it instead of tea at breakfast. It is a thinner, less sweet version of lassi.

| Serves 2 | Preparation: 5 minutes |
|---|---|

¼ tsp cumin seeds

Pinch of salt

¼ tsp sugar (optional)

125 ml / 5 fl oz natural low-fat yogurt

Heat the cumin seeds in a dry pan for a few seconds, then grind coarsely. Put the cumin with the salt, sugar, yogurt and 375 ml / 14 fl oz cold water into a blender and whiz for a moment. Pour it into glasses and serve chilled, with a sprig of fresh mint and a sprinkling of ground black pepper.

**Tip**
- Add ½ a seeded, finely chopped chilli.

# Cumin Chiller Jal Jeera जल जीरा

Street vendors and fast-food shacks serve this refreshing, cooling drink all over India. It's an acquired taste but cumin is known to relieve indigestion and soothe a sore throat.

| Serves 2 | Preparation: 4 minutes |
|---|---|

| | |
|---|---|
| 1½ tsp tamarind paste | 1 tsp jaggery *or* brown sugar |
| 400 ml / 15 fl oz cold water | Small pinch of chilli powder |
| ¼ tsp ground cumin | Pinch of ground black pepper |
| Pinch of salt | 2 mint leaves (optional) |

Put all of the ingredients into the blender and whiz. Serve chilled with a sprig of mint.

**Tip**
- If you haven't any tamarind, use the juice of 1 lemon.

# Sweet and Spicy Cocktail
Mittha Cocktail मीठा कोकतेल

Like many spices, nutmeg is alleged to have a subtly aphrodisiac effect. This light cocktail includes a heady mix of nutmeg, cinnamon and vodka.

| Serves 1 | |
| --- | --- |
| 180 ml / 6 fl oz orange juice | Pinch of grated nutmeg |
| 60 ml / 2 fl oz vodka | Pinch of grated cinnamon |

Mix together the orange juice and vodka in a jug, then sprinkle over the nutmeg and cinnamon.

### Tips
- Substitute some of the orange juice with mango juice.
- Replace the vodka with tonic water.

# Sweet Mimosa Mittha Mimosa मीठा मिमोसा

My friend Sudha loves champagne so I made her my version of Buck's Fizz. After a couple of glasses, she would have thought *anything* tasted wonderful!

| Serves 2 | Preparation: 5 minutes |
|----------|------------------------|

100 ml / 4 fl oz orange juice, chilled

100 ml / 4 fl oz mango juice, chilled

100 ml / 4 fl oz champagne *or* sparkling wine, chilled

Pinch of nutmeg

Pour the juices and the champagne into a jug, then into glasses. Grate some nutmeg over the surface of each. Serve immediately.

**Tip**
- Replace the champagne with lemonade or tonic water.

# Spicy Tea Masala Chai मसाला चाय

Indians love to spice everything up, including tea. However, my family drank it plain, and I was introduced to this version by my cousins in west London, the Vermas, who prepared it every day.

| Serves 4 | Preparation: 10 minutes |
|---|---|

4 green cardamoms, slightly crushed

1 tsp fennel seeds

2 cloves

2 cm / 1 in piece cassia bark (optional)

4 tsp sugar (optional)

250 ml / 9 fl oz milk

2 tsp tea leaves or 2 teabags

Boil the kettle. Pour 750 ml / 27 fl oz boiling water into a saucepan, then add all the spices and sugar and simmer for 1 minute. Then add the tea, or teabags, and allow it to infuse for 30 seconds. Stir in the milk and take the pan off the heat. Pour through a strainer, if using tea leaves, into the cups, or discard the teabags. Serve with savoury biscuits.

**Tip**
- If you have none of the spices, use ½ teaspoon of grated root ginger and allow it to infuse for a couple of minutes.

# Spiced Coffee Masala Coffee मसाला कोफी

Coffee is big business in India, particularly in the south where special contests are held in search of the best cup of Mysore coffee. Several processes go into making the perfect blend but I've kept mine as simple as possible.

Preparation: 2 minutes

Make a pot of coffee then drop in 4 slightly crushed green cardamoms and 4 cloves, or a cardamom and a clove per cup. Allow the mixture to infuse for 1 minute. Then strain off or fish out the spices as you pour it. Add milk and sugar if you like.

**Tip**
- Add a tiny piece of root ginger to the brew.

# Glossary

## A

**aam** mango

**achar** the Hindi word for pickle. There are so many, made out of practically any vegetable, and often meat and fish

**adrak** ginger

**ajowan** carom, or tymol seeds

**akhrot** walnuts

**aloo** potato

**alu bukhara** plum

**amchoor/amchur** a mango powder made by drying and grinding raw green mangoes

**ananas** pineapple

**anardana** pomegranate seeds, used ground in Indian savoury snacks

**anda** egg

**angoor** grapes

**anjeer** figs

**arbi** yam

**arhar dal/toor dal** yellow lentils

**atta** wholemeal flour, used for making Indian breads, e.g. chapatis

## B

**badaam** almonds

**badi elaichi** black cardamom

**badi saunf** fennel or aniseed

**baghar** seasoning

**baingan/baigan** brinjal, aubergine, eggplant

**bakri/bakra** goat

**balti** a dish of meat or vegetables, cooked in a heavy wok-style pan with two handles

**bandh gobi** cabbage

**bara jhinga** lobster

**barfi** an Indian fudge-like dessert made from whole milk

**basmati** long-grain rice

**bhara** stuffed

**besan** chickpea flour

**bhaji** vegetable

**bharta** mash or purée. A dish sometimes made with smoked aubergines cooked with tomatoes and onions

**bhatura** leavened dough made of yogurt and white flour rolled into circles and deep fried

**bhindi** okra, lady finger

**bhuna** fried – a process of cooking spices in hot oil

**bhurji** scrambled

**biryani** a pulao dish in which meat is cooked separately then mixed with rice flavoured with saffron

**Bombay duck** a small fish native to the region around Mumbai, dried. It appears on the table as a crispy deep-fried or roasted dish

## C

**chaakoo** knife

**chai** tea

**chaat** a cold dish made out of vegetables, fruit and spices

**chalni** sieve or strainer

**channa** dried chickpeas

**channa dal** yellow split peas/gram lentils

**chapati** wholemeal wheat bread, rolled out into thin rounds and griddle-baked

**chawal** rice

**chawli** black-eyed beans

**chimta** tongs

**chini-shakkar** sugar

**chota pyaz** shallots

**choti elaichi** green cardamom

**curd** yogurt

## D

**dahi** yogurt

**dal/dhal/daal** pulses and lentils

**dalchini** cinnamon

**deghi mirch** Indian paprika – a large capsicum dried and ground to a powder

**dhakan** lid

**dhania** coriander

**dhansak** a dish made with chicken, vegetables and lentils

**doodh** milk

**doodhwala** milkman

**dookan** shop

**dopiaza** a dish made with double the amount of onions in relation to the meat or vegetable

**dosa** a south Indian pancake made with rice flour and lentils

**dudhi** white pumpkin

**dum** an Indian technique for pot-roasting

## E

**elaichi** cardamom

## F

**firni/phirni** an Indian dessert made with rice flour, rosewater and milk

## G

**gaajar** carrot

**gajarella** a carrot-based milk pudding laced with cardamoms

**garam** hot

**garam masala** hot spice

**ghee** clarified butter

**gobhi/gobi** cauliflower

**gol** round

**gosht** meat

**gulab** rose

**gulab jal** rosewater

**gulab jaman** an Indian dessert made from milk, ghee and flour in a rosewater syrup

**gur** jaggery – unrefined cane sugar

## H

**haandi** an earthenware cooking pot

**haldi** turmeric

**halva** sweets made from syrup and vegetables or fruit that are served cold in small squares. Similar to Turkish delight but thicker in texture, they are translucent and come in bright colours depending on the ingredients

**hara dhania** fresh green coriander leaves

**hara pyaz** spring onions

**hari gobi** broccoli

**hari mirch/simla mirch** green pepper

**hing** asafoetida

## I

**idli** savoury round cakes made from ground rice and lentils, which are steamed and eaten with chutney

**imli** tamarind

## J

**jaggery** unrefined cane sugar
**jaiphal** nutmeg
**jalebi** an Indian sweet – whorls of batter deep-fried and soaked in syrup
**jalfrezi** sauté or stir-fry
**jardaloo/khubani** apricot
**javitri** mace – the lacy outer casing surrounding the hard kernel of the nutmeg
**jeera** cumin
**jhinga** prawn
**jowar** barley

## K

**kaaju** cashew nut
**kaala** black
**kaala jeera** black cumin seeds
**kaala miri** black peppercorn
**kaala namak** black salt
**kabuli chana** white chickpeas
**kachori** fried bread stuffed with lentils and beans
**kaddu** marrow
**kadhai/karahi** wide concave vessel for deep-frying
**kadhi** a yogurt-based curry with dumplings made of chickpea flour
**kakri** cucumber
**kaleji** liver
**kalonji** nigella, similar to wild onion seeds
**karchchi** flat metal spoon used for turning ingredients while frying
**karela** bitter gourd
**kari patta** curry leaves
**katori** small serving bowl, placed on a *thali* (large plate or tray)

**kekda** crab
**kesar** saffron
**khajoor** dates
**khara** plain with very few spices
**kharbuja** yellow melon
**keema** minced meat
**kheer** a rich, thick, creamy Indian rice pudding, often laced with green cardamoms, nuts and sultanas
**khopra** dried coconut
**khubani/jardaloo** apricot
**khurzi** a whole chicken or portion of lamb cooked with a spicy stuffing
**khus khus** white poppy seeds used in Indian cooking to give a nutty aroma; sometimes ground with other spices
**kichdi/kichri** a porridge rice dish with yellow split mung beans and butter
**kishmish** raisins/sultanas
**kofta** meat or vegetable balls, deep-fried then cooked in a curry sauce
**korma** braised
**kulcha** leavened white bread
**kulfi** rich Indian ice cream
**kurmura/mamra** puffed rice, used for making savoury snacks

## L

**laddu** spherical Indian sweetmeat
**lal mirch** red chilli
**lasoon** garlic
**lassi** an Indian yogurt drink, either sweet or salty
**laung** clove
**limbu/nimbu** lemon

## M

**machchi/machli** fish
**maida** plain flour
**makhan** butter
**makkai** corn
**makkai ka atta** cornflour
**malai** cream
**mamra/kurmura** puffed rice
**masala** spice mixture
**masoor dal** red lentils
**mattar** peas
**meetha** sweet
**methi** fenugreek
**mithai** sweets
**mooli** radish
**moong / mung** split green gram
**moong dal** mung beans/green gram
**moongfali** peanuts
**murg** chicken

## N

**naan/nan** Indian bread made with leavened dough
**naashpati** pear
**namak** salt
**narangi** orange
**narial/nariyal** coconut
**narial-kus** coconut grater
**nimbu** lemon

## P

**paani** water
**pakora/pakoda** fried battered vegetables or fish
**palak** spinach
**panch phoran** a blend of five spices used in the Eastern regions of India, such as Bengal
**paneer** Indian cheese
**papad** lentil wafers – also known as poppadums

**papeeta** papaya
**paratha** griddle-fried wholemeal bread
**patta gobi** cabbage
**phool gobi** cauliflower
**pista** pistachios
**poha** flaked rice
**poori** deep-fried bread
**pudina** mint
**pulao/pullao** a pilaf made with rice, spices, meat, chicken or vegetables
**pyaz/piaz** onion

## R

**rai/sarson** mustard
**raita** yogurt-based salad
**rajma** kidney beans
**ras malai** a dessert of cheese dumplings in a cream sauce with pistachios
**rasam** a spicy lentil broth made in southern India
**rava/sooji** semolina
**roti** thin, round pancake-like unleavened bread

## S

**saag** greens/spinach
**sabudana** sago
**sabzi** vegetables, or a vegetable preparation
**sambar** a south Indian soupy dish, made with lentils and hot chillies
**samosa** triangular savoury pastries stuffed with vegetables or meat
**sandesh** a Bengali sweet, made from curd and sugar
**sarson** mustard
**saunf** fennel/aniseed
**seekh kebab** sausage-shaped

kebabs, traditionally cooked in a clay oven or *tandoor*

**sev** crisp deep-fried noodles, made from chickpea or gram flour

**sevia/semia** vermicelli

**shahi** royal

**shakahari** vegetarian

**shakkar/chini** sugar

**shammi kebab** minced-meat kebabs shaped into patties

**sharbat** fruit drink

**shorba** soup

**shrikhand/srikhand** a sweet dish, made with yogurt, sugar and spices

**simla mirch** capsicum/bell pepper

**sirka** vinegar

**sooji/rava** semolina

**soonth** dry ginger

**supari** betel nuts

# T

**tadka** tempering, with spices

**tala** deep-fried

**tamatar** tomato

**tandoor** clay oven

**tandoori** food cooked in a *tandoor*

**tari** gravy

**tava** griddle

**tej patta** bay leaves

**tel** oil

**thali** metal dinner plate

**tikka** chunks of meat cooked on skewers

**til** sesame seeds

**toor/arhar dal** yellow lentils

**tulsi** basil

# U

**urad dal** black lentils

# V

**vindaloo** a Goanese dish made with red chillies, garlic and vinegar

# Z

**zafran** saffron

# Suppliers and Links

Some addresses, telephone numbers and websites for ordering Indian ingredients. For more information, weblinks, tips and recipes, visit www.britspice.co.uk or www.manjumalhi.co.uk

Exotic Spice, Unit 32,
24–28 St Leonard's Road,
Windsor,
Berkshire SL4 3BB
Tel: 07000 785838
Fax: 07000 795939
www.exoticspice.co.uk

Bristol Sweet Mart,
80 St Marks Road,
Bristol,
BS5 6JH
Tel: 01179 512257
www.sweetmart.co.uk

Chillies and Spices by Post
www.chilli-willie.co.uk

www.shop4spice.com

# Acknowledgements

Thank you to my mother, Kami, for her encouragement, and my uncle Raj, for his enthusiasm; my brother Meno, for making those trips back and forth for the sake of spices; Werner van Peppen, for making those trips back and forth for the sake of fresh coriander; to Aditya Khatri, Sudha and Chandrika Kaviraj and Naomi Ramanaden for helping me organize myself, and being great guinea pigs; Arun Ram, Baba Radha Charandas, Mee-Yan Cheung Judge, Pamela Goss, Pauline Barrett, and Abha and Bill Adams, for giving me the drive and determination; Ian Barclay, Neil Sexton, Neely Sood, Lopa Kothari, Patrick Walker, Ben Edwards, Robin Barrett, Rosemarie Macdonald and Jill Franklin for putting up with my moaning and down-days. A big thank-you to Allis Moss, Sandy Maeer and Nick Vaughan-Barratt at the BBC, and talent nurturers Martine Carter, Borra Garson and Michelle Wadsley for believing in me; to my editor, Lindsey Jordan, and publisher, Tom Weldon, at Michael Joseph, for taking the plunge. Thank you to Ami Smithson, with her eye for design, Saskia Janssen, Catherine Lay, Ellie Smith, Jess Ward, Nicola Milner and Sarah Day, and to Hazel Orme for her meticulous copy-editing; to Robert Hutchinson, Tom Sykes and Richard H. Smith at FilmFour for being so accommodating. Also thanks to Tania Ahsan at *Tandoori* magazine; John Davies at Tamarind Fine Foods; Simon Edwards at Cobra Beer; Pedro Carvalho at Media Moguls; and Olivia Grove at Head First.

A juicy thank-you to Sunny Fruit and Veg in Harrow; Nick at Bahasa; Pam Bewley at Magimix; Bharati at In 'n' Out Trading; and Sonu P. Lalvani at Yatra.

# Index

almond
   biscuits 165
   and saffron milk 170
apricots: creamy apricot dessert 157
asafoetida xvii
aubergine, roasted 74
avocado: chilli and avocado dip 154

bacon rice 113
baked beans
   balti 94
   jacket potato filling 144
bananas
   semolina dessert with 158
   *see also* plantains
barbecued food
   chicken in a hot, sweet 'n' spicy
     marinade 140
   chicken satay bites 141
   corn-on-the-cob with couscous
     salad 142
   lamb kebabs 138
   safety tips xxxi
   tikka kebabs 139
basmati rice 108
bay leaf xviii
beans
   curried broad 105
   green beans with ginger and
     mustard 70
   Indian bean hotpot 104
   masala runner 71
beef madras 56
beer: chicken korma with 33

bhaji
   garlic, chilli and mushroom 146
   onion 145
biscuits
   almond 165
   cumin 166
black pepper: simple okra with 76
bread 107, 115–18
   and butter pudding with papaya
     and saffron 156
   chapatis 117
   cheese on toast 21
   deep-fried 118
   naan 115
   peshwari naan 116
   spicy 26
breadcrumbs xxviii
broad beans: curried 105
bubble 'n' squeak, Indian-style 24–5
butter
   chilli and garlic 154
   lentils 95
   spinach 69
   *see also* ghee
buttermilk 171

cabbage with coconut and dried red
   chilli 66
cakes: chocolate cake with cardamom
   and pistachio 164
caraway seeds xviii
cardamom xviii–xix
   chocolate cake with cardamom and
     pistachio 164